# Magna Carta and the Tradition of Liberty

# CONTENTS

Produced by the American Revolution Bicentennial
Administration, the U.S. Capitol Historical Society, and
the Supreme Court Historical Society as a public service.


Copyright © 1976, the United States Capitol Historical
Society and the Supreme Court Historical Society,
Washington, D.C


Library of Congress catalogue number 76-9244


International Standard Book Number 0-916200-12-4

*Cover: King John cedes Magna Carta in 1215; patriots
present Declaration of Independence in 1776. Front endsheet:
Magna Carta (Cotton ms. Augustus II, folio 106). Back
endsheet: Declaration of Independence, from engraving by
William J. Stone.*

# Magna Carta
## and
# The Tradition
## of Liberty

by
Louis B. Wright

# Preface by
# the Lord Chief Justice of England

The travellers from England who founded America brought with them the common law of England. What else could they do? They knew no other law, and were bound to follow that which they knew.

Now, 200 years have passed in which each of our countries has been free to develop in its own way, and it would have been no surprise if our respective laws, and the principles on which we administer justice, had taken different shapes during those years. But this has not happened. The striking fact is not that our laws and law-making have become so different, but that they have remained so very much the same.

For this wholly satisfactory state of affairs, as I believe it to be, much of the responsibility rests on Magna Carta. The Great Charter was the keystone of the arch comprising the English common law. From it are derived those simple sounding principles which are of the very essence of freedom under the law: "No freeman shall be imprisoned...save by the judgment of his peers or the law of the land." "To no one will we sell, deny or delay right or justice."

A country fortunate enough to have its legal system based on such principles would not be anxious for change, and this has proved true of the United States of America, whose written constitution often bears a striking resemblance to the language of Magna Carta—as in the 5th Amendment where it is provided that no one shall be deprived of life, liberty or property, without due process of law. Those at Runnymede who wrangled over the terms of the Charter could have had no idea that they were legislating not only for centuries ahead, but for populations yet undreamed of: "They builded better than they knew."

Perhaps the most vivid present-day illustration of these developments is to be found in the right to habeas corpus. Any man who is detained, or imprisoned, against his will, whether by the police, government agency, or private individual, can be the subject of an application for habeas corpus. Since the applicant's imprisoned state will usually prevent him from making an oral application to the Court, in person, the application is often made by a friend or relative on his behalf. The most common form of habeas corpus was "habeas corpus ad testificiendum" which required the gaoler to have the body (habeas corpus) of the complainant brought before the Court so that the Judge might pronounce on the legality of the detention, and, if this were found to be unjustified in law, to set the applicant free.

At least once a week my Court in London is required to set aside whatever else it may be doing in order to hear an application for habeas corpus, which application, since it concerns the liberty of the subject, must be given priority over all else. In the United States of America the procedural steps may be different, but the substance is the same. Magna Carta serves to rule our respective countries in the jet age, and may we all be duly thankful for it.

*Lord Chief Justice Widgery*

# Preface by the Chief Justice
## of the United States

The extraordinary care free people take to preserve original documents like Magna Carta, the Declaration of Independence, and the Constitution symbolizes the profound concern we have for the substance of what was written on those great occasions in 1215, 1776, and 1787.

Magna Carta, like our own Declaration, was a beginning, not an end, for in the meadow at Runnymede the new rights spelled out were only for a few. But slowly and surely time extended those rights to many. That document is important to people everywhere, but its particular significance to Americans was that in 1776 it gave a solid legal basis for the claim that what the colonists sought—indeed demanded—were their rights as Englishmen, as defined in Magna Carta and refined for more than 500 years after that. They demanded only their due.

The Due Process concept embraced in our Constitution traces directly back nearly 600 years to Runnymede. It is more than a technical legal concept for it pervades our Constitution, our laws, our system, and our very way of life—that every person shall be accorded what is *due*.

When we honor the Declaration in this Bicentennial year we also pay tribute to Magna Carta from which it sprang and to those who for nearly six centuries pressed to enlarge and expand for all people the rights declared at Runnymede for a few. Their struggle epitomizes the nature of humankind, striving to prove that men and women were meant to be free.

Just as time extended the reach of Magna Carta, it has also expanded the meaning of the Declaration and the Constitution so as to include all people and to exclude none. Today in our country, as in England, no person is above the law and all are equal as to its burdens and its benefits. This is what is meant by Equal Justice Under Law.

*Chief Justice Burger*

*Architect Osman's heraldric design for Magna Carta case*

# Introduction by
## John W. Warner, Administrator
### American Revolution Bicentennial Administration

On the steps of the United States Capitol building in the spring of 1974, I was privileged to receive the oath of office as Administrator from Gerald R. Ford, then Vice President of the United States. He called upon me to solemnly swear that in the discharge of my duties I would "support and defend the Constitution of the United States."

Although I had made this affirmation many times before, as do all assuming positions of public trust, this oath had a special significance. For now I would be encouraging citizens across our nation to reaffirm the Declaration of Independence, the Constitution, and the Bill of Rights as the main themes of their community Bicentennial planning. Combined, these classic instruments have provided Americans with a system of government which has survived every test and remains the oldest continuous form of a democratic republic on earth today.

As the ceremony concluded, a thought crossed my mind: for the Bicentennial, would it be possible to bring to this Capitol building that document which originally inspired many of the basic guarantees found in our government—the 1215 Magna Carta? Today, there still exist four originals of that great charter, two of them in the cathedral churches in which they were originally deposited—the Lincoln and Salisbury—and the other two in the British Museum. Of the latter, one bears some marginal notes, possibly in the hand of King John, attesting to the intensity of the confrontation with his barons. This unique original, perhaps the most historically valuable copy, has never left England; would it come to honor the birthday of our great Declaration?

I recalled the impressive Magna Carta ceremonies at Runnymede in 1957 which drew distinguished lawyers, judges, scholars and statesmen, from all over the world including the United States. Through the media, millions then shared in the dedication rites of the American Bar Association's memorial to the great landmark of freedom under law. How noble it would be for the enduring symbol of Magna Carta to bear witness to the solidarity and continuity of human dignity and freedom of Americans by coming to our nation's Capitol.

That historic event had inspired an early, unsuccessful attempt to secure the loan of an original copy. In 1965 Earl Warren, Chief Justice of the United States, convened in the Nation's Capitol a symposium of international jurists and lawyers under the auspices of the World Peace Through Law Conference. As a member of his Executive Committee, I was asked to create an exhibit of copies, perferably originals, of important legal documents from all over the world. Bearing letters from our Chief Justice, I visited the hierarchy at Lincoln Cathedral and at Salisbury Cathedral seeking to borrow Magna Carta—but to no avail. Likewise, the British Government declined an original, but they graciously provided a copy of a later issuance of Magna Carta, dated 1225. This was placed on exhibit at the National Archives alongside the Declaration of Independence. The experience convinced me that to obtain an original would take the combined spirit of the people of both nations.

In January 1975, I was given the opportunity to express the enthusiasm of the people of the United States for their Bicentennial to the people of the United Kingdom through their British Bicentennial Liaison Committee. The chairman of the Committee, Lord Lothian, hosted a luncheon in my honor during which there was a lively discussion concerning the many plans being considered for participation in the Bicentennial. At an appropriate moment, I suggested that consideration be given to a loan of one of the four remaining originals of the 1215 Magna Carta.

This seed of thought sprang to life within the Committee; ultimately it produced a special motion from the British Parliament. Joining in these efforts were Sir Peter Ramsbotham, the British Ambassador to the United States, the Honorable Elliot Richardson, U.S. Ambassador to the Court of St. James, and Mr. John Morgan, Head of the Cultural Relations Department of the British Foreign and Commonwealth Office. In response to the motion passed by the Parliament on July 2, 1975, Her Majesty Queen Elizabeth gave directions authorizing the loan of Magna Carta 1215 to the people of the United States.

Subsequently, I received the kindest letter from Sir Peter Ramsbotham, British Ambassador: "This announcement appears to have caught the imagination of both our peoples. The British Liaison Committee is much indebted to you for this excellent idea, which has from the beginning had widespread appeal. I should like to express to you our warmest thanks for putting forward the suggestion. 1976 is indeed going to be a momentous year."

The people of the United States and the people of Great Britain having joined in spirit, the final arrangements were left to the respective leaderships of Parliament and the Congress. Assisting in the arrangements, and particularly in making this book available to the general public, are the combined efforts of the American Revolution Bicentennial Administration, the U.S. Capitol Historical Society and the Supreme Court Historical Society. Commencing in June 1976, an original of Magna Carta 1215 will be resting in the rotunda of the Capitol Building of the United States. It stands there as a testament to the accomplishments of Americans over 200 years in preserving for themselves and for others throughout the world the basic principles of human dignity and freedom.

That Magna Carta had a profound influence upon the draftsmen as they devised our system of government between the years 1776 and 1789 is an accepted fact. Just how much, is a question for Dr. Louis Wright, distinguished author of this book, and for other historians to answer.

However, as the Bicentennial marks the 200th anniversary of the adoption of the Declaration of Independence, I close with the observations of Thomas Jefferson, the acknowledged principal author, on the relationship between these two landmarks of freedom. In the twilight of his great career, controversy arose over the originality of the language used: did the Declaration capture the thoughts of great philosophers from classical and medieval times or was it simply a re-statement of ideas that had been debated within the Congress just before its adoption?

On the eve of his death, Mr. Jefferson in letters (based upon notes he had made at the time of the drafting) forthrightly proclaimed the document to be reflective of both traditions and the will of the people. He wrote:

> "Whether I had gathered my ideas from reading or reflection, I do not know. I only know that I turned to neither book nor pamphlet while writing it...it was intended to be an expression of the American mind."

The American people will be everlastingly grateful to Britain and Parliament for bringing Magna Carta to them.

*ARBA Administrator Warner*

# I

## THE
## TREASURED
## SYMBOL

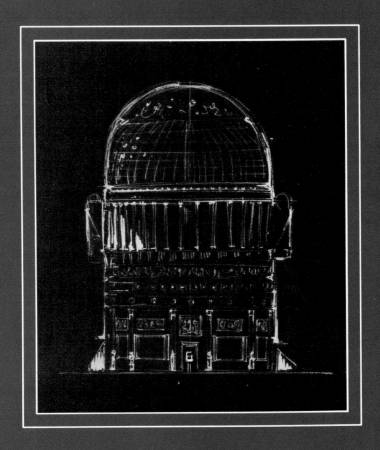

# F

rom the time of the first permanent English settlement on this continent, the Virginia settlement in 1607, Americans have placed their faith in a long tradition of law to preserve their liberties. The colonists looked back to a legacy from Magna Carta as their basic inheritance of freedom and justice.

When the present site of Washington, D.C. was still part of the endless wilderness, and the plantations a few miles away were not yet free from the dread of marauding Indians, settlers were consulting among themselves about the common law that was their heritage. William Fitzhugh, a planter of Stafford County, then a frontier region in Virginia, was busily providing legal advice to his neighbors and friends; he cited as his authorities the ancient writers and Magna Carta, the basic charter granted by King John in 1215. The colony of Virginia, like other English settlements in North America, was not yet blessed with professional lawyers; literate men, with small but useful libraries, sought legal wisdom from English writers on the law. Always there was recourse to the authority of Magna Carta, based on some interpretation that the settler might find among his handful of books.

Fitzhugh's letters provide valuable clues to the application of the rule of law in Virginia. Writing in 1679 to Richard Lee about statute and common law, Fitzhugh asserted that statute law cannot be properly interpreted without a knowledge of the common law, and common law "is only to be learned out of ancient authors (for out of the old fields must come the new corn) contrary to opinion of the generality of our judges and practicers of the law here."

In a letter to Thomas Clayton on April 7, 1679, he cited Sir Edward Coke's *Institutes* and other landmark works, and supported his argu-

---

*A precious gem in the vast setting of the Capitol rotunda, the Magna Carta exhibit at the center of the main floor (opposite) was designed by Architect Louis Osman.*

*Holding Magna Carta,*
*a patriot fights for liberty*
*on Massachusetts' first state seal.*

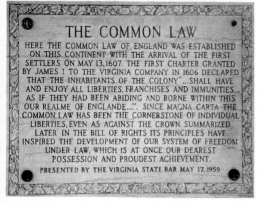

*America's early settlers believed their rights as Englishmen stemmed from Magna Carta. At left above, Pilgrims read the Mayflower Compact; their Massachusetts Bay Charter declared they should "enjoy all liberties and Immunities of free and natural Subjects." At left, a plaque at Jamestown commemorates the introduction of common law on these shores.*

ments with quotations from Cicero and Magna Carta. The Great Charter of King John, through its many reinterpretations over the centuries, had become a symbol of freedom under law to Englishmen everywhere—even to those colonists clinging to the fringe of a vast new continent.

At the very end of the seventeenth century, when Sir Francis Nicholson, an arbitrary governor of Virginia, undertook to throw some of the colonists into jail without due process of law, he was taken to task because he had violated the provisions of Magna Carta. "Some of those have taken the liberty to tell him that such proceedings were illegal and not to be justified in any country that had the happiness to be governed by the laws of England," reported Robert Beverley, the historian. "To whom he has been heard to reply that they had no right at all to the liberties of English subjects, and that he would hang up those that should presume to oppose him, with Magna Carta about their necks."

These displaced Englishmen in America had little if any concept of the restricted significance of the original charter wrested by the barons from King John at Runnymede in June, 1215. By the late seventeenth century, Englishmen everywhere, at home and abroad, had come to believe that Magna Carta was their palladium of liberty, the basis of funda-

mental rights that we now take for granted.

The spot chosen for the culminating negotiations between King John and the barons was Runnymede, a green meadow along the Thames between Windsor Castle and the town of Staines. Today it is still a meadow where children play and fly their kites while their elders, when the summer weather is fine, picnic and revel in a spot of sunshine. Because the English are not given to cluttering the landscape with historic monuments, Runnymede remains a pleasant park. An unobtrusive museum exhibits facsimiles of documents suggesting the significance of the locale. In 1957 the American Bar Association dedicated a simple memorial at Runnymede, and on June 13, 1965, it held a symbolic meeting there to celebrate the 750th anniversary of the Great Charter. Lawyers on both sides of the Atlantic have promoted an annual gathering of the Magna Carta Society. But the meadow itself has remained almost undefaced with ill-considered monuments, a tribute to the good taste of the English.

From its first day to this, Magna Carta has become a symbol magnified far beyond the dream of any baron of the thirteenth century. American colonists, determined to assert for themselves the rights of Englishmen, made much in their Revolutionary arguments of the liberties traceable to Magna Carta.

11

Significantly, so great was the Old Dominions's reverence for the tradition of the common law going back to Magna Carta that in 1965 the state created The Magna Carta Commission of Virginia to celebrate its own 750th Anniversary of the Great Charter. This commission published a series of booklets explaining the background, meaning, and enduring values of the Charter.

Because English-speaking people on both sides of the Atlantic continue to trace the ancestry of their liberties back to the charter granted by King John in 1215, it is a mark of international good will that the United Kingdom should send to this country on loan one of the two copies preserved in the British Library (the library portion of the British Museum is now called the British Library).

The copy of Magna Carta on exhibition in the Rotunda of the Capitol is one of the two copies from the manuscript collection of Sir Robert Cotton, long preserved in the British Museum and classified as "Cotton Manuscript Augustus II, 106." Who first owned it is unknown. Sir Robert Cotton acquired it in 1629, the gift of a friend, Humphrey

A 19th century view of King John
consenting to Magna Carta (opposite,
above) gives little idea of the beauty of
Runnymede meadow where that encounter
took place in 1215. The meadow is glimpsed
in the scene above, with the American Bar
Association's memorial in the foreground.
The historic document, displayed for the
Bicentennial year in the U.S. Capitol (left),
normally resides in the British Library
(opposite), once part of the British Museum,
which was founded in 1753 (left, below).

13

*Other copies of the 1215 Magna Carta can be found in England's Salisbury and Lincoln Cathedrals (above left and right respectively). The "Golden Passage" of Magna Carta (below) is strikingly reflected in the Fifth Amendment of the U.S. Constitution (opposite, below).*

**N**o freeman shall be taken, imprisoned, disseised, outlawed, *or in any way destroyed, nor will we* proceed against him or *prosecute him, except* by the lawful judgment of his peers, and *by the law of the land.*

MAGNA CARTA
Chapter 39

Wyems. It is a handsome copy and contains corrections probably made during the discussions between King John and the barons. The British Library's other copy of the 1215 manuscript, listed as "Cotton Charter XIII, 31A," was literally "snatched from the burning," for it was damaged in the fire that swept the Cottonian Library in 1731. Eventually both copies came into the possession of the British Museum along with other manuscripts from Sir Robert Cotton's library. The damaged copy has a fragment of the Great Seal still appended, the only copy with any portion of the seal still attached. This copy also has emendations probably made during the discussions at Runnymede, but damage by the fire all but destroyed its legibility.

The Lincoln Cathedral copy of the 1215 Magna Carta and the Salisbury Cathedral copy are both in good condition and show less haste in the copying than the two copies in the British Library. In fact the Lincoln copy was chosen for facsimile reproduction in an engraving authorized by the Public Record Commissioners in 1810.

The document now on exhibition is regarded by scholars as the most authoritative copy extant. The British nation has sent to Washington a manuscript revered as an ikon of incalculable value so that visitors during this Bicentennial year can see the most enduring symbol of our inherited liberties—liberties common to the free and independent people of both Great Britain and the United States.

*no person shall be held to answer for a capital, or otherwise infamous crime, unless on a presentment or indictment by a grand jury..., nor shall any person...be deprived of life, liberty, or property, without due process of law...*

CONSTITUTION OF
THE UNITED STATES
Amendment V

## II

## THE
## CROWN AND
## THE LAW

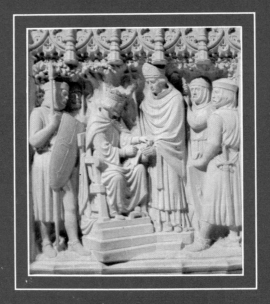

The unwritten constitution that governs the British people has grown through the ages by slow accretion. The accumulation of precedents, the agreements of sovereigns with their subjects, a diversity of written charters, and tacit understandings between governors and the governed have created a constitutional system that has been the envy of other freedom-loving peoples. This system would be difficult to imitate and impossible to duplicate because of its ancient and complicated origins. Many volumes on the subject have been written by learned authorities on the history of law and politics, and scant justice can be done this theme in a few pages. Nevertheless a brief account may help Americans to comprehend the significance of a fundamental document in the long development of a system of government that has had a profound influence upon our own destiny.

When William, Duke of Normandy, invaded England in 1066 to seize from Harold, last of the Saxon kings, a crown to which he had scant claim, he brought with him from France certain principles of government which he grafted upon such Saxon laws as he chose to retain. Already in France the feudal system had become established. That is to say, the ruler at the top of the pyramid of power had under him lesser powers, all of whom, in descending order down to the small land holder, peasant, and serf, owed allegiance and service to the rank next above him.

In a lawless age, the need of the weak for protection of the strong had resulted in this development. A local lord with landed estates would lease his holdings to lesser folk who promised service and produce for rights to farm the land—and for the protection that went with it. The lord himself had probably received his estates

*The front panel of the Canterbury Pulpit in Washington's National Cathedral shows King John agreeing to Archbishop Langton's and the barons' terms as expressed in Magna Carta.*

A map of England on the brink of the Norman Conquest in 1066 shows the country's many divisions. The invaders from Normandy landed at Pevensey, fought and won near Hastings. When William the Conqueror's later heir King George III yielded independence to the U.S. in 1781, his arms (above) still bore the French words "Dieu et Mon Droit"–God and My Right.

from some greater baron or from the sovereign, to whom he was obligated to furnish a stated number of men-at-arms and knights equipped for battle. The sovereign frequently granted what was called an "immunity" to permit barons, in place of the sovereign's officers, to dispense justice in their own courts. At the bottom of the social heap, the small farmer had to supply labor to work a stated number of days on his overlord's estate. The lowest farm laborers—serfs (or villeins, as they were called)—were attached to the land and could not leave it. Feudal practices were so varied and complicated that a volume would be required to detail the characteristics at different times and in different localities. But the essence of feudalism was graduated service which each order of society owed to the next above it. Irregularities in the practices in different times and places, however, were so great that feudalism could hardly be called a "system." One noted English historian has called feudalism in England after William the Conqueror a "regulated anarchy." Nevertheless, the feudal hierarchy introduced by the Conqueror changed English society and altered the course of legal progress.

In 1066, England lay ready for a strong "man-on-horseback" to take control. It was not yet a united or a homogeneous realm. The Saxon King Alfred had ruled in Wessex, consisting of most of southern England south of the Thames. Central and eastern England had been conquered by the Danes. The "wild Welsh" occupied the green mountains and valleys west of an earthwork called "Offa's Dike" running from a point just west of Chester to the Severn River. More than a century after Alfred, a Christianized Dane, King Canute (1016-1036), established briefly a maritime empire in collaboration with Scandinavia, but lines of communication were difficult to maintain, and his dream of a northern empire failed under incompetent successors.

In 1042 Edward, later called "the Confessor," a weakling, managed to regain the throne for the Saxons. Edward was more priest than ruler, and though the clergy in time called him "saint" for favors to them and for the beginning of Westminster Abbey, he prepared the way for the Norman conquest by filling high offices with Normans. When he died in January 1066 without an heir, Harold, Earl of Wessex, seized the crown. William, Duke of Normandy, asserting that he had a better claim, landed at Pevensey on October 1, 1066, with some 5,000 mounted knights and some 6,000 foot soldiers. Two weeks later, on October 14, he met Harold on a hill a few miles northwest of Hastings. Harold's army fought bravely but it was no match for William's charging knights, supported by archers. By nightfall Harold and his bravest men lay dead and Saxon rule

*England's King Harold is cut down by a Norman knight's broadsword in this scene from the contemporary Bayeaux Tapestry.*

in England was forever ended.

William lost no time in subduing the conquered land. In the south, Saxon nobles submitted without much resistance. Within a few weeks London, already the largest and strongest city, sent word of its submission and invited William to be crowned in Westminster Abbey. The event, on Christmas day, took place amid a sudden tumult that William put down with severity. When rebellion broke out in the north, three years after his coronation, William marched through Yorkshire, Durham, and Cheshire, laying waste the countryside and slaughtering whole villages. Gradually he stamped out sporadic rebellion and at length reigned supreme from Scotland to the Channel.

To hold the land in check, the Conqueror parceled out territories to his barons, whose obligation it was to erect fortifications and garrison them with their knights. The former inhabitants found themselves mere vassals of the new possessors. The fortifications consisted of castles that were at first wooden structures on huge earthen mounds surrounded by palisades and perhaps moats. Later the country would be dotted with more permanent stone castles.

Norman churchmen swarmed over from France and began the erection of great abbeys and cathedral fortresses, the best surviving example being Durham Cathedral. Near Hastings, to commemorate

his victory, William founded Battle Abbey. The churchmen, as did the barons, engrossed vast holdings of lands and in time became very rich. Since they were not expected to supply a quota of vassal-knights to the sovereign, they paid money into the royal exchequer and supplied civil officials for the king.

To insure complete subjugation–and thorough taxation–William in 1086 ordered a complete survey and census of his realm, the results of which are preserved in the famous Domesday Book, one of the greatest sources of information about medieval England.

Because William liked to hunt, he turned enormous tracts into royal forests. He and his successors took over nearly a third of the land for hunting, and the Forest Laws were among the most obnoxious and tyrannical that his subjects had to endure. A countryman might be executed for killing a stag, or suffer mutilation for poaching in the rabbit warrens. The game laws of England, which lasted until modern times, were an affliction that began with the Normans.

Although the Conqueror began the practice of permitting local issues to be decided by baronial courts, he kept a firm grip on the reins of justice and maintained the royal prerogative throughout the land. To assert the king's authority, he appointed a

*Before the Norman Conquest, English law was marked by neither mercy nor equity. Above, a Saxon witan, or councilor, decrees a hanging.*

sheriff in each of the counties, an office that carried dignity and authority, often occupied by a nobleman appointed—and removable—by the sovereign. In America we have appropriated the name "sheriff" but that office bears little resemblance to the sheriff in England in medieval or later times.

The unruly barons whom William brought with him from France were not always content to keep the peace and submit to the king's orders. Their greed prompted a rebellion in 1075 which William put down with his usual severity. Even so strong a ruler as the Conqueror, however, had to avoid alienating too large a proportion of the populace. To save themselves from recurring rebellion, his successors in the next generation were driven from time to time to grant charters specifying certain liberties to their subjects. These charters marked the beginnings of the realization that even a sovereign had to recognize the dominance of law. William the Conqueror, it is true, gathered power into his royal hands and centralized government under the sovereign, but he laid the foundation for the slow development of constitutional rights as well.

His reign saw the beginnings of long controversies over the respective roles of church and state in the administration of justice. William installed an Italian cleric from Padua, Lanfranc, as archbishop of Canterbury. Lanfranc had a keen legal mind, and it was largely owing to his influence that William worked out a compromise which separated secular and ecclesiastical courts. In ecclesiastical courts, the pope's canon law ran; in the secular courts, the king's law, now developing into what would be known as the common law, prevailed. One other type of law had some influence in the spiritual courts: the civil law, embodied in the Code of Justinian, was dominant on the continent and taught in the universities of Bologna and Padua and later at Oxford. The jurisdictions of the ecclesiastical and secular courts were not always clearly differentiated, and this led to controversy. After much bickering, William maintained the right to nominate bishops to be elected by the cathedral chapters, but the pope retained the right of their spiritual investiture. Herein lay seeds of the dispute which led to upheavals in the reign of King John.

Powerful as the Conqueror was, he dared not attempt to rule without some restraint. For the first time, it is true, the whole realm was brought under one centralized royal authority, but that authority was hedged about by embryonic constitutional controls. In a striking passage, George Macaulay Trevelyan sums up the situation: "The Conqueror . . . successfully prevented England from falling into the anarchy of political feudalism prevalent on the continent. . . . But he did not enjoy unlimited despotic power, nor by right did anyone who ever succeeded him on the throne of England. William was doubly bound by law—by the old Saxon laws which he had ostentatiously sworn to observe, and by the feudal customs of continental Europe to which his followers from overseas were one and all devoted. It was from the marriage of these two systems that in the course of long centuries the laws and liberties of

*Since the late 13th century, English laws have been made in Parliament. An early view of its members meeting appears on the Parliamentary Seal above.*

*England's Parliament has been a model for legislatures in other democratic countries. Here, the Queen at State Opening of Parliament in 1974.*

modern England were evolved."

No parliament yet existed in England. That would be a gradual development in after years. But William did consult his chief barons and the great churchmen of his time, men who made up an informal council wherever the sovereign happened to be. Later, from such beginnings, developed the Privy Council, the Court of King's Bench, and finally, Parliament.

William the Conqueror of course had retained his overlordship of Normandy after 1066. The fact that successive English monarchs sought to retain or gain vast territories in France was the source of endless wars that often threatened the stability of the English throne.

When William died in 1087, he left the English crown to his second son William, called Rufus because of his red hair, and the duchy of Normandy to his first son Robert, perhaps an indication of his conception of the relative value of the two domains. A third son, Henry, inherited Norman estates which he held in fief to his brother the duke, who in turn owed nominal allegiance to the French king.

None of William the Conqueror's sons possessed his capacity to rule. William Rufus, motivated by insatiable greed, soon alienated the English barons by his extortions. None mourned when a fellow huntsman in the New Forest let fly an arrow that killed him. The slayer assured all who cared to listen that he mistook the king for a deer. At any rate, William Rufus's brother Henry, who at once seized the crown, clearly regarded the accident as a happy event

and favored the huntsman and his family. Henry's reign was undistinguished but he did improve England's fiscal system, establish the office of the exchequer, and bring about a more orderly process of collecting the royal revenue. Henry also made an important contribution to the administration of justice by creating orderly courts under judges sent throughout the kingdom at regular intervals to hear pleas of the crown.

Despite fathering a horde of bastards, Henry I had only two legitimate offspring—a son William who drowned after a drunken brawl at sea, and a daughter Matilda. Although Matilda was the legitimate heir to the crown, England was not yet ready for a queen. Civil war broke out when Stephen, son of Henry I's sister Adela, was crowned. Stephen was a weak king, and his reign, from 1135 to 1154, was a period of civil war and confusion. Utilizing their opportunities, the barons gained back much of the authority that they had been forced to concede to Henry I. The civil war between Matilda and Stephen eventually resulted in a compromise in which Stephen agreed that Matilda's son Henry, by her husband Geoffrey Plantagenet, Count of Anjou, would be named his heir. A year after this agreement, Stephen conveniently died, and Henry II, first of the Plantagenet kings, came to the throne. A strong king, he would bring order to England and institute many reforms.

Henry II, king of England and possessor of rich territories in France, in 1152 took to wife Eleanor, Duchess of Aquitaine, whose marriage to Louis VII

A time for chivalry and crusading, the 13th century witnessed such courtly scenes as knights pledging their faith (opposite) and receiving their trappings from the ladies (left). It also saw brutality, as when King John's crusading brother Richard I slew hostage Saracens, whose heads appear with him above.

of France had recently been annulled. Eleanor, a remarkable woman in any age, was too independent and full of spirit to be compatible with the monkish king of France. Her new husband, Henry of England, was more to her liking but their union was less than peaceable, and she spent the later years of their marriage as his prisoner of war. But before she had permanently alienated Henry, she had borne him five sons and four daughters, pawns in the chess game of power politics in the twelfth century. Her youngest son was John, later to become King John.

This was the period of the crusades, of the quixotic efforts of Christians of western Europe to wrest and hold the Holy Land from the hosts of Islam, even if they had to wade in blood to the Sepulchre. While still married to Louis of France, Eleanor had accompanied her pious spouse on the second crusade. Her son, Richard I of England, called Coeur-de-Lion, was a gallant leader in the third crusade.

The noted English historian George M. Trevelyan, in summarizing the advances made in England under Henry II, comments: "Of all the monarchs who have worn the island crown, few have done such great and lasting work as Henry Plantagenet, Count of Anjou. He found England exhausted by nearly twenty years of anarchy.... He left England with a judicial and administrative system and a habit of obedience to government which prevented the recurrence of anarchy, in spite of the long absences of King Richard and the malignant follies of King John." Perhaps Henry's most important contribution to the world we have inherited was the foundation he laid for Magna Carta—the rights guaranteed to the barons by his son John.

Henry II made great strides in reforming judicial procedures. By appointing a bench of royal judges and sending them into every shire to hear cases, he brought about a body of "judge-made law," or what in later times came to be understood as the "common law." Older legal customs were superseded. In Saxon and early Norman times, cases might be decided by ordeals of several sorts: casting an accused into water that had been blessed by a priest; if guilty, the water would reject him and he would float; if innocent, the water would receive him and he would sink. Another ordeal was by hot irons. Sometimes cases were decided by combat. These barbarous methods were gradually abandoned as Henry's judges and his assizes developed a rudimentary jury system.

At first juries did not hear evidence and decide on the facts presented; they were, instead, called to testify about facts already known to them. Under Henry we can discern the beginning of the grand jury. Twelve men chosen from each district called a "hundred" were sworn to present to the king's court evidence of wrongdoing in that particular district. The beginnings of the petty jury can be seen in a later system of having twelve men testify under oath as to the truth in cases concerning disputes over property. The evolution of juries into bodies hearing evidence instead of merely testifying about facts known to them was a gradual development, but the seed had been sown in Henry's judicial reforms.

Feudal obligations of the barons to supply a certain number of knights to fight in the king's wars were also modified by Henry. His wars were for the most part in France, where he had continually to fight to retain his dominion over semi-independent political divisions. English barons would not willingly supply knights to fight in foreign wars. Henry ingeniously devised a plan to substitute for knights a cash payment called "scutage," meaning literally "shield money." This enabled him to hire merce-

naries for his wars across the Channel. Later, King John's exorbitant demands for scutage helped to bring on the crisis that resulted in Magna Carta.

Henry II's greatest legal struggle was with the church. He had made the tactical mistake of appointing as archbishop of Canterbury his chancellor and close friend, Thomas Becket. A warrior-priest, Becket had fought in Henry's wars in France and had supported his taxation of church property. Henry fully expected collaboration from the new archbishop. That he did not get. Now independent and the servant only of God, Becket became a thorn in Henry's side. When the king proclaimed the Constitutions of Clarendon (1164), which attempted to define the relations of church and state, Becket refused to give his approval. After years of wrangling, Henry, according to legend, cried out, "Who will rid me of this troublesome priest?" Four of his knights rode to Canterbury and murdered the archbishop in the north transept of his cathedral. In 1172, within two years of his death, Becket was canonized and almost immediately Canterbury became a holy city for pilgrims to visit.

One of the contentions between Henry and the church had been over the jurisdiction of lay or ecclesiastical courts in cases involving "criminous clerks" (clerks charged with crime). Henry maintained that clerks who committed felonies "should be accused first in the lay court, then handed over to the Church court for trial, and, if condemned and de-

graded from holy orders by their spiritual superiors, should finally be brought back by the King's officers to the lay court for sentence and punishment." After Becket's martyrdom, the king found it expedient to admit defeat and to leave the trial and punishment of clerics to the church. For centuries to come, men who could read and write (the accomplishment that marked a "clerk" in medieval times) could claim "benefit of clergy" and often escape serious punishment.

Although Henry II had to make compromises in his conflict with the church, the struggle to define the limits of ecclesiastical authority were continued in later reigns, particularly in that of his son, John.

Henry II's last years were marred by rebellions, wars, and treachery within his household. Eleanor conspired with her sons to seize the French realms and make them independent of Henry. Worst of all, the king's heir and namesake plotted against his father with the young king of France, Philip Augustus, nominal liege-lord of the Plantagenets. Rebel though young Henry was, his father was desolated when he died of a fever. To prevent Eleanor from aiding her rebellious sons, Henry locked her up in Salisbury Tower and subsequently moved her about to various other prisons. There she stayed until 1189 when, embittered and defeated, Henry died in France shortly after he had "taken the Cross" to go on the third crusade. Henry had accomplished much for England, but the necessity of fight-

*Thomas Becket, Archbishop of Canterbury, is killed by king's knights in this illumination from the 1200s. After his martyrdom, Becket's shrine at Canterbury became a target for pilgrims. They wore his image (above) about their necks.*

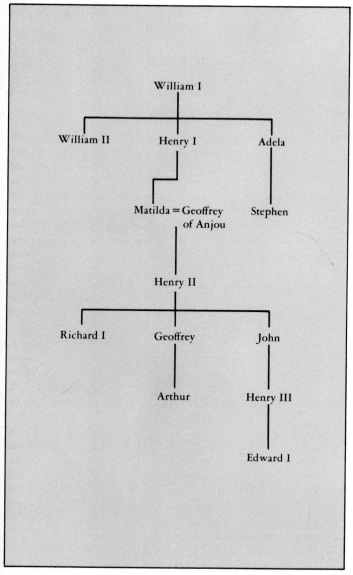

```
                        William I
          ┌─────────────────┼─────────────────┐
    William II         Henry I              Adela
                    ┌──────┘
          Matilda = Geoffrey              Stephen
                    of Anjou
                        │
                    Henry II
          ┌─────────────┼─────────────┐
    Richard I       Geoffrey          John
                        │               │
                     Arthur         Henry III
                                        │
                                    Edward I
```

*Henry II, first of the Plantagenet Dynasty, had to quell his sons' rebellion in order to retain his hold on the crown.*

ing for the Plantagenet domains in France had been his ruin, as it was to be the ruin of his heirs.

For ten years, from 1189 to 1199, Richard Coeur-de-Lion reigned over England but did not rule, for he preferred fighting infidels in Palestine or contending for Plantagenet lands in France. Actually he spent less than a year in England. Returning from Palestine, he was thrown into prison in Austria by some of his fellow crusaders and held for ransom. Henry of Hohenstaufen, Emperor of the Holy Roman Empire, was enormously pleased at Richard's capture, as was Philip Augustus of France. Richard, who had outshone them all as a knight in shining armor in Palestine, had naturally incurred the jealousy and fear of rival crusaders. As the darling of the pope, he also was a potential defender of the papacy against such enemies as the emperor, who was involved in a controversy with the church. Hence Henry of Hohenstaufen was determined to hold him as long as possible and ransom him only for the utmost treasure. Meanwhile, in England and Normandy, Richard's treacherous brother John was stirring up rebellion. He tried to persuade his mother Eleanor, who now held the balance of power between her two surviving sons that, since Richard would never come home, he (John) ought to be declared king of England and duke of Normandy. Eventually, however, Richard was released. After much devious negotiation with the emperor—and the collection of a huge ransom in silver—Eleanor, accompanied by a group of hostages, journeyed to the emperor's court and redeemed her son.

Although Richard was a romantic figure in his own time, he was virtually useless as even a nominal ruler. In an attempt to satisfy his brother John, known in his youth as "Lackland," he turned over to him several counties, with permission for him to rule them without remitting any taxes to the royal treasury. This was a reversion to feudal practices that Henry II had tried to abolish.

Richard, however, had left the realm of England under the care of a capable justiciar, an officer who served as vicegerent for the king—Hubert Walter, archbishop of Canterbury. Walter wisely fostered the growth of towns and granted them charters which guaranteed privileges that were treasured in years to come by the rising middle classes. These charters for little towns held the greatest promise for constitutional development made during the reign of Richard Coeur-de-Lion.

When, in 1199, Richard died from an arrow wound received in one of his French wars, John Lackland at last came into his own. That is, he gained the crown of England. But throughout his reign he wasted his substance, and that of his English subjects, fighting for French possessions. His insistent demands for increased scutage—and other tyrannical exactions—at last drove the most powerful of his English barons to rebellion. That rebellion brought on the confrontation in the meadows of Runnymede in June, 1215. And on that momentous occasion, King John was forced to seal the charter that became known as the Great Charter, safeguard of English liberties.

*King John's seal (above) was affixed to early copies of Magna Carta.*

Riding to the hounds, King John exults in his favorite sport. Less heroic than his brother Richard, he was nonetheless skilled, dynamic, and determined to preserve royal rights.

Effigy of King John in Worcester Cathedral vividly portrays that fiery monarch.

# III

## CONFRONTATION
## AT
## RUNNYMEDE

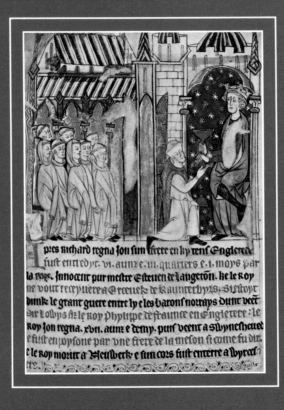

By the autumn of 1214, King John had succeeded in making enemies throughout his dominions and faced a new rebellion of the barons of England. The reasons for his difficulties were numerous. Although historians are agreed that he was a more efficient monarch than his popular brother, Richard Coeur-de-Lion, his efficiency was largely motivated by his greed and his need for money to wage war in France. He contrived systematic ways of raising funds, often made personal inspections (rudimentary audits, we might say) of the exchequer, and sometimes presided over royal courts of justice. Observing the increasing prosperity of the country gentry and the towns, he was eager to improve the collection of revenue for the crown by new forms of taxation and additional demands for scutage from the barons. Because taxation by any name is always unpopular, John found this policy a certain way of multiplying his enemies.

In personality, King John was ruthless and cruel. He seduced the wives and daughters of his subjects and was not averse to having enemies who thwarted him tortured and murdered. He was believed to have slaughtered with his own hands his young nephew, Arthur, Duke of Britanny, for fear that Arthur would press a claim to the throne of England. Although Shakespeare wrote a play about King John that never mentions Magna Carta, the dramatist made capital out of Arthur's murder, as did many of John's own subjects. Describing the pastimes of medieval Europe, Sidney Painter once commented that "King John of England considered a hanging a suitable after-dinner entertainment."

In an age that admired personal courage above administrative efficiency, King John won no plaudits. He was never seen at the head of

---

*Disdained by the clergy because of his fight with Archbishop Langton and the barons, King John was once thought to have been poisoned by a cup a monk had handed him.*

his troops, and he acquired the unflattering sobriquet of "John Softsword." He was also an inveterate loser. At the battle of Bouvines in 1214, the Emperor Otto of the Holy Roman Empire, allied with John against Philip Augustus of France, was utterly routed, and all of Normandy not already in Philip's possession fell to the French King. The king of England had by this time lost, in addition to Normandy, all of Maine and Anjou. With Poitou virtually in anarchy, John could no longer count on a foothold there. The English held only parts of Aquitaine in the south, including the strategic port of Bordeaux.

As if he did not have enemies enough, John, as early as 1205, had embroiled himself in a long and bitter controversy with Pope Innocent III. The complicated quarrel grew out of the appointment of a new archbishop of Canterbury after the death of Hubert Walter, the statesman-archbishop who had administered the kingdom in the absence of Richard Coeur-de-Lion. King John nominated a favorite of his own but a faction of the cathedral chapter voted for another. In this dilemma, the pope declined to approve either candidate and suggested to the English delegation sent to Rome that the chapter elect Cardinal Stephen Langton of York, an ecclesiastic learned in canon law. The chapter duly elected Langton, and the pope consecrated him without King John's approval, which aroused the king's unbounded rage. After John had seized church property and abused some of the monks, the pope placed England under an interdict and in 1209 excommunicated the king. As John had little religion and no fear of damnation, he cynically enjoyed the immense church revenues diverted into the royal treasury.

Conditions changed abruptly in 1213 when John learned that Philip Augustus was preparing to invade England and appropriate the crown technically

*At Runnymede the barons presented John with their famous Articles (top) which preceded Magna Carta. Robert FitzWalter, one of the barons, is represented by the seal above. Following in that vigorous tradition, Simon de Montfort (on stained glass window, left above, led his fellows in the Barons' War of 1263-67, which was won by King Edward I (shown opposite with Parliament). Edward issued a confirmation of Magna Carta in 1297: taxes could only be imposed with consent of Parliament.*

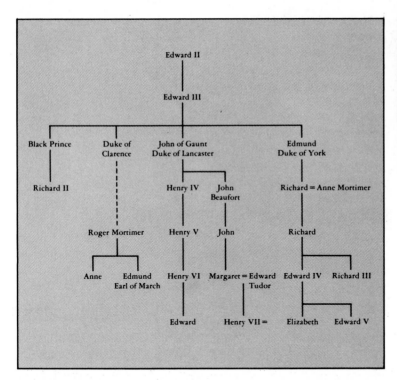

Edward II

Edward III

| Black Prince | Duke of Clarence | John of Gaunt Duke of Lancaster | | Edmund Duke of York |
|---|---|---|---|---|

Richard II

Roger Mortimer | Henry IV | John Beaufort

Richard = Anne Mortimer

Anne | Edmund Earl of March | Henry V | John | Richard

Edward | Henry VI | Margaret = Edward Tudor | Edward IV | Richard III

Edward | Henry VII = | Elizabeth | Edward V

made vacant by John's excommunication. The time had come for the king of England to make peace with the pope. This he accomplished by accepting Stephen Langton as archbishop of Canterbury and promising to return sequestered money and property to the church. More important than this, John offered to submit England to the pope and swore allegiance to the papacy as the pope's vassal. An English king could go no further. John had thus created a situation that would vex English sovereigns until Henry VIII severed all ties with Rome.

If King John hoped that he would win the undivided support of the new archbishop of Canterbury, he was mistaken. Stephen Langton became the mediator between the rebellious barons and the obstinate king. Some historians have maintained that he was the author of the most statesman-like clauses in Magna Carta. There is little doubt that he proved a wise counselor, listened to—not always with complete amity—by both barons and the king. It is possible that he was responsible for demanding reforms broader than the aggrieved barons at first had intended. During most of the early part of 1215, when England was plagued with civil strife between barons and king, Langton played an influential role in negotiations which led to Magna Carta and the promise of peace.

When King John and the barons agreed upon beautiful Runnymede as a place for meeting, they were not looking for a flowery meadow: more sinister reasons dictated their choice. Runnymede was convenient to King John's favorite residence, Windsor Castle, on the south side of the river; it was also

convenient to Staines, north of the river, where the barons made their headquarters. Because they had the Thames between, they were both in a reasonably defensive position, protected from surprise attack on their flanks by marshland on either side of the meadow. For this was a grim meeting, with armed warriors on each side. Though they had come under truce, experience had made them mutually distrustful.

If Hollywood were screening the scene of June 15, 1215, at Runnymede, we would see the flower of medieval chivalry on gaily caparisoned horses riding to meet one another, lances flying pennons and the sun glinting from burnished steel. Striped tents of the barons would cluster in the background, while a silken pavilion in the foreground would be made ready for King John to seat himself and stamp his seal on the historic document. All this would be pure fiction.

Unfortunately, no eye-witness of the events bothered to write down a detailed description of the scene, but we can be sure that gallantry and splendor were absent. Historians have long debated what really happened at Runnymede. A tent was probably available for discussion by the principals; King John and his retainers undoubtedly rode back to Windsor for the night, while the barons retired to lodgings at Staines. There is no proof that King John set his seal to Magna Carta at Runnymede on June 15. It was evidently sealed sometime later.

Debate between the barons and the king and his advisors went on for several days. Obviously, on June 15 King John agreed to the critical issues, but

*Regarding Magna Carta as a pillar of his policies, Oliver Cromwell (right) led England after the beheading of Charles I (above). Charles had refused to accept a constitutional monarchy, as expressed in Coke's 1628 Petition of Right. Vowing they would abide by the Bill of Rights, William and Mary (opposite) were installed after the Glorious Revolution of 1688.*

details had to be worked out during the next few days. J. C. Holt, an English historian, in his book *Magna Carta* comments: "It seems, therefore, that the drafting of final terms took at least four days, and indeed monastic writers later recorded that there had been much discussion and negotiation to and fro."

The king and the barons, apparently on June 19, reached an agreement by which "peace was made and sworn." This oath was the culmination of debate. Concerning the legalization of the Charter, Holt observes: "King John did not sign Magna Carta; there is no evidence that he could write. He did not even seal it; sealing charters was the task of the spigurnel, a member of the Chancery staff. Furthermore, there is no evidence at all that the Charter figured in the ceremonies at Runnymede either on 19 June or on any other day. There is no evidence that there was some kind of solemn and ceremonial sealing of an 'original' Magna Carta. There is not even any evidence that such a sealed original ever existed: all that survive are four charters, two of which reside in the counties to which they were sent in 1215; and there is no evidence that any sealed engrossment of the Charter was available before 24 June when the first seven were delivered for distribution."

Although not all historians agree precisely with Holt about what happened, or did not happen, at Runnymede, he summarizes the opinions of many modern scholars. They point out that Magna Carta

followed the conventions of the time for the preparation and distribution of royal charters. The essential happening at Runnymede was the agreement reached between king and barons, an agreement confirmed by oath. This oath, Holt emphasizes, "gave immediate authority to the terms of agreement. The Charter, in contrast, was a record which provided evidence for those not present at Runnymede and for generations yet to come of what had been agreed. It is for this reason that the Charter, in the view of modern authorities, has come to be 'disengaged from the recorded ceremonial of 19 June'." The surviving copies of Magna Carta, dated 1215, are as valid and symbolic as if King John had sat in his tent that day and sealed them with his own hand.

We can be certain that the provisions set down in Magna Carta represent the distillation of weeks and perhaps months of discussion among the rebellious barons, modified at Runnymede by the necessity of compromise with the king. A document now commonly called "The Articles of the Barons" enumerates many of the grievances against the king and evidently was drawn up prior to the beginning of discussion with the king at Runnymede. Magna Carta, as finally drafted, set down in a single document the undertakings and reforms that the king accepted. Twenty-five barons were chosen to serve as a sort of court to see that the king observed the conditions he had sworn to keep. A list of these barons, as given by Holt, follows:

"Richard, Earl of Clare, William de Fors, Earl of

Aumale, Geoffrey de Mandeville, Earl of Gloucester, Saer de Quenci, Earl of Winchester, Henry de Bohun, Earl of Hereford, Roger Bigod, Earl of Norfolk, Robert de Vere, Earl of Oxford, William Marshal, junior, Robert FitzWalter, Gilbert de Clare, Eustace de Vesci, Hugh Bigod, William de Mowbray, the Mayor of London, William de Lanvallei, Robert de Ros, John de Lacy, Constable of Chester, Richard de Percy, John FitzRobert, William Malet, Geoffrey de Sai, Roger de Montbegon, William of Huntingfield, Richard de Muntfichet and William de Albini of Belvoir."

What really was Magna Carta and why has it endured? It was not a treaty between king and barons but a charter of privileges granted by the sovereign in perpetuity. King John's immediate successors on the throne reissued the Charter, sometimes modified, but always containing its most important guarantees. It remained a primary document indicating that law was above the king.

But Magna Carta is more than that. Although some scholars have argued that greedy barons had merely wrested from an unwilling king a charter assuring them of a continuance of vested privileges, the Charter contains promises of new rights to free men throughout the land, at least as certain paragraphs of the Charter came to be interpreted. Whether King John or the barons were themselves conscious of the implications of some of the statements, one may wonder.

It is pleasant to speculate that Stephen Langton inserted significant phraseology that has had enduring values to later generations. Some authorities believe that Langton had a major part in drafting the Charter. Evidence for this belief may be the anger displayed by Pope Innocent III over sections of Magna Carta that curtailed the power of his recently acquired vassal, King John. In his rage, the pope on August 24 declared the Charter null and void and pronounced excommunication upon anyone who observed or tried to enforce its provisions. Furthermore, he ordered Archbishop Langton to Rome— exiled from the see of Canterbury. But both Innocent III and King John had only a short time more to live, and their own actions were soon null and void. John died on October 19, 1216, and a revised version of the Great Charter was issued less than a month later, on November 12, by the government of the new king, nine-year-old Henry III.

Four copies of King John's Magna Carta, bearing the date June 15, 1215, survive. Fair copies were made and sent to each of the counties and perhaps to important towns. Provision was made for their preservation in important strongholds and in the archives of cathedral churches. All but the four surviving copies perished in the centuries after 1215. Two of these copies are in the British Library, one is in Lincoln Cathedral, and the fourth is in the cathedral at Salisbury. The Lincoln manuscript was exhibited at the New York World's Fair in 1939 and was returned to the United States during World War II for safekeeping. The copy being lent to the United

*Another legacy from Magna Carta, England's Habeas Corpus Act was passed in 1679 (right).*

States for the Bicentennial celebration is the more legible of the two copies in the British Library. Scholars regard it as perhaps the most authoritative version because it has marginal corrections which they think represent revisions made during the debate between the king and the barons, revisions incorporated in the fair copies.

The surviving copies are all written in one continuous format without paragraphing the incorporated articles. Printed versions list the articles in numbered sequence for ease of reference. Article 1 declares in unequivocal language "for us [King John] and our heirs in perpetuity, that the English church shall be free, and shall have its rights undiminished and its liberties unimpaired," a statement that gave great comfort to the men of the English Reformation. This article concludes: "We have also granted to all the free men of our realm for ourselves and our heirs forever, all the liberties written below, to have and hold, them and their heirs from us and our heirs." This large and generalized statement was ambiguous enough to please everybody. Precisely what "liberties" were granted "to all the free men of the realm" were subject to varied interpretations as time wore on. We must remember that the language of King John's Charter meant something entirely different to Henry VIII, to Sir Edward Coke, to John Locke, and to the American colonists. For example, "free men" in King John's charter were freeholders of land, not free and independent men of later ages.

Many of our most cherished liberties derive, it was believed by later generations, from Article 39,

which reads: "No free man shall be taken or imprisoned or disseised [have his property taken from him] or outlawed or exiled or in any way ruined, nor shall we go or send against him, except by the lawful judgment of his peers or by the law of the land." This article too was sufficiently broad—and vague—to permit almost any interpretation. Men have seen in Article 39 the germ of trial by jury, habeas corpus, and other fundamental freedoms now regarded as our natural rights. When these have come into question, our ancestors could invoke Magna Carta and cite this article. The Charter also contained clauses that granted more freedom to women, especially widows, and guaranteed certain property rights. A succinct analysis of the Charter with an interpretation of the provisions relevant to later ages is provided by A. E. Dick Howard in a booklet, *Magna Carta, Text and Commentary,* published by the University Press of Virginia in 1964. The Charter was a wonderful document which lawyers could invoke to sustain almost any freedom.

The reissue of the Charter by Henry III immediately after John's death was only one of many confirmations which Henry and later sovereigns found it expedient to make with such alterations as suited them. In 1217 came a second reissue by Henry III and a reissue in 1225 became the form which later generations knew best and used. Of the 1225 reissue William F. Swindler in *Magna Carta, Legend and Legacy* comments: "The Charter of Liberties was once more subjected to editing—from John's sixty-three chapters it had gradually been tightened up

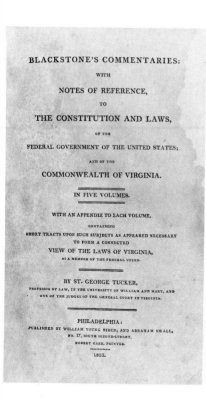

BLACKSTONE'S COMMENTARIES:

WITH

NOTES OF REFERENCE,

TO

THE CONSTITUTION AND LAWS,

OF THE

FEDERAL GOVERNMENT OF THE UNITED STATES;

AND OF THE

COMMONWEALTH OF VIRGINIA.

IN FIVE VOLUMES.

WITH AN APPENDIX TO EACH VOLUME,

CONTAINING

SHORT TRACTS UPON SUCH SUBJECTS AS APPEARED NECESSARY
TO FORM A CONNECTED
VIEW OF THE LAWS OF VIRGINIA,
AS A MEMBER OF THE FEDERAL UNION.

BY ST. GEORGE TUCKER,
PROFESSOR OF LAW, IN THE UNIVERSITY OF WILLIAM AND MARY, AND
ONE OF THE JUDGES OF THE GENERAL COURT IN VIRGINIA.

PHILADELPHIA:
PUBLISHED BY WILLIAM YOUNG BIRCH, AND ABRAHAM SMALL,
NO. 17, SOUTH SECOND-STREET.
ROBERT CARR, PRINTER.
1803.

into thirty-seven." Swindler adds: "Ten years after Runnymede, Magna Carta had settled into the foundations of English government, a cornerstone later to be covered over and forgotten in the rubble of fifteenth and sixteenth century strife, but to be uncovered again in the making of the modern nation."

So long as Henry III was guided by William Marshall, Earl of Pembroke, and other wise counselors, the kingdom remained reasonably peaceful, but after he came of age and took the reins of government into his own hands, unrest increased until in 1258 civil war broke out. A faction led by Simon de Montfort, Earl of Leicester, won a victory in 1264 over the royal forces at Lewes. De Montfort had enlisted popular support of members of the emerging middle class, some of the knights and country gentry, and the lower orders of the clergy. After his victory, he called together an assembly consisting of the knights of the shire and two members from each of the chartered towns to advise on his policies, Thus Simon de Montfort is given credit for fostering the development of Parliament, which took more concrete form in the reign of Henry III's son and heir, Edward I. De Montfort, who died the next year fighting for his cause at the battle of Evesham, has been glamorized beyond his deserts for this constitutional development, but from that time onward, no king of England could claim to be above the law of the land. Abuse of the royal prerogative would perpetually remind Englishmen of Magna Carta, and the people, represented in Parliament, would make themselves heard.

*Sir William Blackstone, the great interpreter of English laws, was introduced to colonial America by St. George Tucker (top), the title page of whose classic work appears at left above. Tucker served as professor of law at Virginia's William and Mary (above).*

# IV

## MAGNA CARTA's
## ENDURING
## INFLUENCE

$\mathcal{E}$very general history of England and almost every book which has ever appeared on English law has had something to say by way of commentary on Magna Carta" asserted William S. McKechnie in *Magna Carta: A Commentary on the Great Charter of King John.* Interpretation and comment on the provisions of Magna Carta began with the earliest writers on the law after the issuance of the Great Charter. Most famous of these was Henry of Bracton (died 1268), justice of what came to be called the Court of King's Bench. His compilation of court decisions had an enormous influence on the development of common law. Versions of Bracton, and of other medieval commentators, especially those known only as "Fleta" and "Britton," were cited by colonial Americans in trying to reach decisions based on English legal traditions. These early commentators helped to keep lawyers and the literate public aware of the significance of Magna Carta, or at least of their interpretations of it.

Until the eighteenth century, knowledge of Magna Carta was based on Henry III's third issue of 1225, which was reissued by Edward I in a version identified, by its first word, as *Inspeximus.* This word, meaning "we have read" showed that Edward had read the charter. The reissues, of course, did not represent accurately King John's Charter, for they were altered and modified versions of the original. The first printed version appeared in October 1499 from the press of Richard Pynson, the king's printer. Many printed versions followed, but not until William Blackstone's scholarly edition of *The Great Charter and the Charter of the Forest,* 1759, did the public have available King John's Great Charter of 1215. Blackstone discovered and collated the two copies of the manuscript in the Cottonian collection in the British Museum. His edition and his *Commentaries,* pub-

---

*In drafting a Frame of Government for Pennsylvania in 1682, scholarly William Penn (shown in this primitive painting presenting a treaty to the Indians) drew upon the principles of Magna Carta.*

VIRGINIA

lished in 1765 and many times thereafter, gave to both Englishmen and Americans a more accurate knowledge of medieval law and of the common law of England than any had possessed before his works appeared.

The glorification of Magna Carta as the fundamental document in the evolution of the common law of England was the work of Sir Edward Coke (pronounced Cook), the great protagonist of the common law and opponent of the supremacy of the royal prerogative in the reign of the first two Stuart monarchs. Before Blackstone, no one had a greater influence upon the interpretation of English law on both sides of the Atlantic than Coke. Made Chief Justice of the Court of Common Pleas in 1606, he was elevated, against his vigorous protest, to be Chief Justice of the Court of King's Bench in 1613. Coke knew that in the Court of Common Pleas he had greater influence in promoting the common law—and richer fees.

Coke's interpretations of Magna Carta, based on the issue of 1225, derived from his own ingenuity, motivations, and imagination. His elaborate exposition of the Great Charter, long to influence English jurisprudence, occurs in the second of four *Institutes*, or commentaries on the law. But this *Second Institute*, presenting vigorous arguments against the royal prerogative, was hidden away and not published un-

til 1642 by order of the revolutionary Long Parliament, eight years after Coke had died at the age of eighty. The Parliamentarians found in it justification for their fight for freedom from the absolutism of King Charles I.

Just as modern jurists find the federal Constitution of 1787 a flexible document and are able to invoke interpretations that the "Founding Fathers" could not anticipate, so Coke read into Magna Carta interpretations that coincided with his views and prejudices. The words of Magna Carta meant something to Coke that would have amazed King John and the barons of the thirteenth century. "Although this commentary, like everything written by Coke, was long accepted as a work of great value, its method is in reality uncritical and unhistorical," remarks McKechnie. "The great lawyer reads into Magna Carta the entire body of the common law of the seventeenth century of which he was admittedly a master." Anachronistic though Coke's commentary may have been, it had an enduring influence and was invoked in constitutional crises in times to come. In 1628 Parliament and King Charles I reached an impasse over a demand by Parliament for a reaffirmation of Magna Carta with additions that the king refused to accept. These additions were designed to assure freedom from imprisonment without cause and to guard against unjust levies and

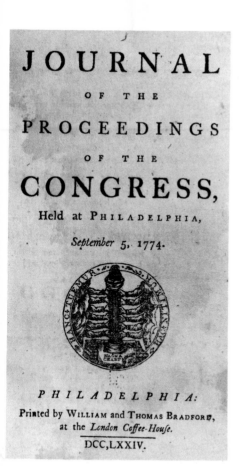

# JOURNAL

### OF THE

## PROCEEDINGS

### OF THE

## CONGRESS,

Held at PHILADELPHIA,

September 5, 1774.

### PHILADELPHIA:

Printed by WILLIAM and THOMAS BRADFORD,
at the London Coffee-House.

DCC,LXXIV.

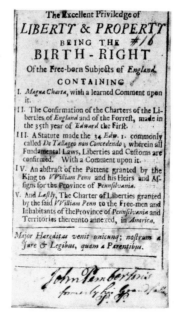

The Excellent Priviledge of
LIBERTY & PROPERTY
BEING THE
BIRTH-RIGHT
Of the Free-born Subjects of England.
CONTAINING

I. Magna Charta, with a learned Comment upon
it.
II. The Confirmation of the Charters of the Liberties of England and of the Forrest, made in
the 35th year of Edward the First.
III. A Statute made the 34 Edw. 1. commonly
called De Tallageo non Concedendo; wherein all
Fundamental Laws, Liberties and Customs are
confirmed. With a Comment upon it.
IV. An abstract of the Pattent granted by the
King to VVilliam Penn and his Heirs and Af-
signs for the Province of Pennsilvania.
V. And Lastly, The Charter of Liberties granted
by the said VVilliam Penn to the Free-men and
Inhabitants of the Province of Pennsilvania and
Territories thereunto annexed, in America.

Major Hæreditas venit unicunq; nostrum a
Jure & Legibus, quam a Parentibus.

*Patrick Henry attacked royal privilege in pleading
"The Parson's Cause" in 1763 (opposite). Today
Americans recall his later "Give me Liberty or Give
me Death!" When aroused patriots gathered in
Philadelphia for the First Continental Congress in
1774, their journal was imprinted with a colophon
supported by Magna Carta (left). Knowledge of that
ancient document was imparted to Americans by such
works as Penn's Liberty and Property (above).*

taxation by the crown. After much wrangling, Parliament and king agreed upon a technical compromise termed a "Petition of Right." Coke's interpretation of Magna Carta served as a clinching
argument. Swindler observes that the Petition of
Right "was to be developed by subsequent circumstances into one of the building blocks of the modern constitution." He also comments that Parliament's victory over the king resulted in Charles I
ratifying "Parliament's (and Coke's) interpretation
of the Great Charter."

In Parliamentary debates leading to the enact-
ment of the Habeas Corpus Act of 1679, and in the
subsequent enactments during and immediately after the so-called Glorious Revolution of 1688,
Coke's commentary on Magna Carta continued to
serve as authority from "ancient law." On February
13, 1689, William and Mary agreed to the Declaration of Rights, and a little later in the same year, Parliament shaped the Declaration into a statutory Bill
of Rights.

That Coke should have such an influence is a tribute to his own learning in the ancients, even if he
did interpret them for his own purposes. He paid
tribute to the great writers about the law who had
preceded him: Bracton's *Of the Laws and Customs of
England,* Sir John Fortescue's *De Laudibus Legum
Angliae (In Praise of English Law),* Sir Thomas Little-

ton's *Tenures* (which Coke was to edit and revise into one of his own most important works), and many others. Furthermore, Coke searched available legal records from the time of Edward IV onwards. All this research resulted in his *Institutes* and his great compilation of law cases normally referred to simply as *Coke's Reports*. Witten in law French, with a preface in Latin, the first part of the *Reports* appeared in 1600, and over the years until 1659 thirteen volumes were published. *Coke's Reports* became the great authority on the common law, used on both sides of the Atlantic. If colonial libraries in Virginia, New England, and elsewhere had few other books, they usually had *Coke's Reports* and the *Institutes,* which informed them of their rights as Englishmen inherited from the past, back to 1215 and Magna Carta.

Myth sometimes can exert a more profound influence than fact. It is not always what happened that counts but what men *believed* happened. "There is scarcely one great principle of the English constitution of the present day, or indeed of any constitution in any day, calculated to secure national liberties, or otherwise to win the esteem of mankind, which has not been read by commentators into the provisions of Magna Carta," states McKechnie. "In particular the political leaders of the seventeenth and eighteenth centuries discovered among its chapters every important reform which they desired to introduce into England, thereby disguising the revolutionary nature of many of their projects by dressing them in the garb of the past." McKechnie quotes Edmund Burke as claiming that Magna Carta even created the House of Commons! From the seventeenth century to the present day, the myth of the significance of the Great Charter has had an abiding

influence upon English and American beliefs about the source of our liberties.

Coke's version of Magna Carta affected the thinking of Americans and the laws they adopted. Colonial Americans were dogmatic in their belief that they enjoyed "all the rights of Englishmen," and that those rights embraced all the liberties confirmed by Coke's interpretation of Magna Carta and the common law. In the era of controversy that preceded the War of Independence, the authorities in London denied that colonists could claim the same rights as subjects of the king domiciled in Great Britain. Even Blackstone held the view that the inherited rights of Englishmen were not automatically conveyed across the Atlantic. But colonials, hard to convince that they had forfeited those rights by emigrating, continued to look back to the ancient writers for confirmation. Faith in Magna Carta is reflected in their laws and their proclaimed liberties.

As the settlers of Virginia, the first colony, were eager to adopt laws based on English common law, so even in Massachusetts Bay, a colony early dominated by the Puritan clergy, the ruling element wanted to shape its statutes as nearly as possible in conformity with English models. John Winthrop, the governor, wrote in 1635 that the General Court decided "that some men should be appointed to frame a body of grounds of laws in resemblance to a Magna Charta [the usual spelling of Carta in the seventeenth century], which... should be received for fundamental laws." A little more than a decade later, in 1646, some disgruntled citizens petitioned the General Court for redress because Massachusetts Bay had departed from English precedents in some of its laws. The General Court published an answer,

*Violence flared in the colonies as England sought to gain taxes by selling stamps like the one above, an action Americans deemed in violation of their "rights as Englishmen." The contemporary skull and crossbones at left above caught the mood of the day. Opposite, New Englanders hang a stamp master in effigy.*

with provisions of English law, beginning with Magna Carta, in columns parallel with related provisions in the Massachusetts statutes.

All of the English colonies looked back to Magna Carta as the source of fundamental liberties, which they had inherited. Before the Declaration of Independence, when colonials were arguing that they had all the rights of Englishmen, they constantly invoked Magna Carta. This reverence for the Great Charter began early, as we have seen.

Maryland is an example of the persistence of the appeal to Magna Carta. "Within the first ten years of the colony's life, at least four attempts were made to put on the statute books of Maryland statements of the rights of Englishmen, specifically the guarantees of Magna Carta," A. E. Dick Howard points out in *The Road from Runnymede: Magna Carta and Constitutionalism in America.* This work provides an excellent synthesis of the influence of the Great Charter, from the earliest of colonial times to the impact of traditional concepts on modern interpretations of due process and other legal inheritances from the common law of England. Maryland, as Howard shows, continued to cite Magna Carta until the outbreak of the War of Independence.

Similar attitudes toward the Great Charter prevailed in other colonies. Maryland, the Carolinas, New York, and New Jersey "serve to illustrate," says Howard, "the extent to which the ancient statute of Magna Carta" had become imbedded in the legal consciousness of colonial Americans. "Magna Carta was being absorbed into the lifeblood of English America much in the way in which it had become an accepted feature of private and public law in England in the Middle Ages."

43

THE PATRIOTIC AMERICAN FARMER.
J-N D-K-NS——N Esqr. BARRISTER at LAW:
*Who with Attic Eloquence and Roman Spirit hath Asserted,*
*The Liberties of the BRITISH Colonies in America.*

*'Tis nobly done, to Stem Taxations Rage,*
*And raise, the thoughts of a degen'rate Age,*
*For Happiness, and Joy, from Freedom Spring;*
*But Life in Bondage, is a worthless Thing.*

*Printed for & Sold by R. Bell, Bookseller.*

William Penn, friend of the Stuarts though he was, utilized Coke's Magna Carta in his own defense when he and William Mead in 1670 were brought to trial in England for "tumultuous assembly," that is for preaching Quaker doctrine. Penn declared that he based his rights on common law, that law guaranteed by the Great Charter as confirmed by Henry III in 1225 and by later sovereigns. Although the jury was browbeaten, threatened, and eventually fined when it brought in a verdict of "not guilty," both the jury and the defendants steadfastly maintained their rights and privileges guaranteed by the Great Charter.

The flouting of the guarantees of the Charter at his own trial made Penn doubly conscious of the importance of that document, and when he undertook to draft laws for his colony of Pennsylvania and of the Quaker colony of West Jersey, he incorporated provisions taken directly from Magna Carta. More than that, in 1687 he saw to the publication in Philadelphia of a commentary on the Charter entitled *The Excellent Privilege of Liberty & Property. Being the Birth-Right of Free-Born Subjects of England.* Included was the 1225 text of Magna Carta, its first printing in America. Penn also had a facsimile made of one of the copies of the 1215 Charter in the British Museum and placed it in the archives of Pennsylvania. Penn was concerned that his settlers might know "what is their natural Right and Liberties." The "Charter of Privileges" that Penn procured for his colony in 1701 incorporated much of the thinking that he had derived from Coke's commentary on Magna Carta in the *Second Institute*—a fact which illustrates the continuing vitality of that great lawyer's influence.

The writings of the Founding Fathers and their speeches frequently cite Magna Carta and Coke's commentary. Many of them of course had Coke's *Institutes* as well as his *Reports* in their libraries. John Adams, who had studied his Coke diligently, was often to refer to Magna Carta and its guarantees in legal arguments and in constitutional debates. As a young man in Braintree, Massachusetts, he had heard a preacher, the Reverend Lemuel Briant, quote Magna Carta "as though he himself had signed it." Later he heard the learned James Otis denounce Great Britain for violating the privileges guaranteed by Magna Carta. Adams himself in arguing against the Stamp Act based his reasoning on privileges going back to Magna Carta. In his *A Defence of the Constitutions of the United States* (1787), he asserted that Americans had drawn on the unwritten British constitution and on Magna Carta.

Thomas Jefferson was less indebted to Magna Carta than Adams and was more inclined to place his faith in natural law. But he himself had studied Coke, a stern discipline he maintained, but one necessary for the training of good lawyers. George Mason's "Declaration of Rights" owed much to the rights which Englishmen had wrung from their sovereigns, beginning with Magna Carta.

After the War of Independence, when the separate states had to draw up constitutions, Magna Carta continued to exert an influence upon legal thinking in America. According to Swindler, nine of the original thirteen states incorporated in their fundamental laws the essence of Article 29 of Coke's version of Magna Carta guaranteeing to every individual "remedy by the course of the law" for "any injury done him in his person or property."

45

*Arguing and politicking their fellow delegates toward Independence, Sam and John Adams (above, top and below respectively) were aided by the support of such legalistic Virginians as Thomas Jefferson (right, above). In the scene set within the draft of the Declaration opposite, the drafting committee (consisting of Jefferson, John Adams, Benjamin Franklin, Robert Livingston, and Roger Sherman) debates the precise phrasing of the famous document.*

Overleaf: *The drafting committee presents the Declaration of Independence to the Continental Congress.*

On both sides of the Atlantic, truths derived through the passing centuries from the interpretation of an idealized Magna Carta have profoundly affected the development of constitutional theories, the unwritten constitution of Great Britain and the written but elastic constitution of the United States. Summarizing his views on the legacy of Magna Carta, Sir Winston Churchill in *A History of the English Speaking Peoples* declared: "The underlying idea of the sovereignty of law, long existent in feudal custom, was raised by it into a doctrine for the national State. And when in subsequent ages the State, swollen with its own authority, has attempted to ride roughshod over the rights or liberties of the subject, it is to this doctrine that appeal has again and again been made, and never, as yet, without success."

Doctrines from the same sources have permeated American legal and constitutional thinking. Volumes would be required merely to cite and analyze all of the references to Magna Carta, Coke and the common law, and their influence. How great has been their impact upon our own constitutional theories and judicial attitudes is a theme for legal historians. We can assert with assurance, however, that no single document has ever had so long and so powerful an influence upon the legal concepts of the English-speaking peoples as the text of the ancient manuscript which Americans now have the privilege of seeing in the rotunda of the Capitol through the courtesy of the United Kingdom.

A Declaration by the Representatives of the UNITED STATES
OF AMERICA, in General Congress assembled.

When in the course of human events it becomes necessary for one people to
dissolve the political bands which have connected them with another, and to ~~as~~
-sume among the powers of the earth the separate and equal ~~station~~ station to
which the laws of nature & of nature's god entitle them, a decent respect
to the opinions of mankind requires that they should declare the causes
which impel them to the separation.

We hold these truths to be self-evident: that all men are
created equal & independent, that ~~from that~~ their creator with ~~equal~~
~~rights~~ inherent & inalienable, among which are the preservation of

life, & liberty, & the pursuit of happiness; that to secure these rights, go
-vernments are instituted among men, deriving their just powers from
the consent of the governed; that whenever any form of government
shall becomes destructive of these ends, it is the right of the people to alter
or to abolish it, & to institute new government, laying it's foundation on
such principles & organising it's powers in such form, as to them shall
seem most likely to effect their safety & happiness. prudence indeed
will dictate that governments long established should not be changed for
light & transient causes: and accordingly all experience hath shewn that
mankind are more disposed to suffer while evils are sufferable, than to
right themselves by abolishing the forms to which they are accustomed. but
when a long train of abuses & usurpations [begun at a distinguished period,
&] pursuing invariably the same object, evinces a design to ~~subject~~ reduce
them ~~to arbitrary power~~ under absolute Despotism, it is their right, it is their duty, to throw off such
~~government~~ & to provide new guards for their future security. such has
been the patient sufferance of these colonies; & such is now the necessity
which constrains them to [expunge] alter their former systems of government.
the history of the present king of Great Britain is a history of ~~unremitting~~ repeated injuries and
usurpations, [among which appears no solitary fact ~~to contradict the uniform tenor of the rest but all~~] to contradict the uniform tenor of the rest, [all of which] have in direct object the
establishment of an absolute tyranny over these states. to prove this, let facts be
submitted to a candid world, [for the truth of which we pledge a faith
yet unsullied by falsehood]

# V

## AN
## ENDURING
## SYMBOL

On July 2, 1975, the following motion was approved by Parliament:

*That an Humble Address be presented to Her Majesty praying Her Majesty will give direction that, to mark the Bicentennial celebrations of the United States of America, there be made on behalf of Parliament to the Congress of the United States, as representative of the American people, a loan for one year of one of the two original 1215 copies of Magna Carta held by the British Library; that a permanent showcase be presented to the Congress for the display of the document, the document to be replaced at the end of the loan period by a replica: that the gift be presented by representatives from both Houses of Parliament...*

The British Bicentennial Committee then faced the question of who should design the resplendent case in which the document would be displayed in the Capitol rotunda. Unhesitatingly they selected Louis Osman, the architect—or, rather, the Renaissance man—who among other things had crafted the crown for the investiture of Prince Charles. A remarkable blend of jewelry, gold, and silver, the crown (pictured on next page) reveals the seemingly magical way in which Osman brings together ancient values and modern skills.

Contemplating the Bicentennial contribution he had been called upon to make, Osman said, "I knew it was a very old document, whose ink had faded, whose vellum was stained, which consisted of 50 lines of tiny medieval script in abbreviated Latin, and measured 19 inches by 14. So it wouldn't mean much to anyone who tried to read it; and in a rotunda 190 feet high and 90 feet across, the poor little document was going to get lost unless one was very careful."

Osman was invited to come to Washington and view for himself the remarkable space in which the display would appear. George M.

---

*In this front view of the glass-topped case on its pedestal in the rotunda, one sees the twice-real-size translation of Magna Carta which rises from the middle of the case.*

White, Architect of the Capitol who was entrusted by the Congress's Speaker of the House with overseeing the arrangements, recalls Osman "...standing there, in the middle of the rotunda, realizing as only a designer would how much attention would naturally be focused right there, at the center of the circle."

"He was worried about the light," Mr. White also remembers, "because the document cannot be directly exposed to the sun. But I pointed out how the sunlight coming into the rotunda through the dome's lower row of windows never travels very far down the walls. The document would be perfectly safe."

The English designer then returned to his Tudor mansion, Canons Ashby, in remote Northamptonshire. There he conceived the secure yet fantastic idea for the exhibit, and there he and his team of craftsmen began to execute it with the skill of jewellers and the proportional finesse of cabinet makers.

The basic plan has been to present the document (or its replica in gold, after the original returns to England) as if it were one page of an opened, medieval volume. Opposite will be an elaborate, symbolic

illumination. And rising up from the center will be a translation of Magna Carta, with large gold letters on glass.

This dazzling creation, cradled in a gold-lined, stainless steel case, will stand above the floor of the rotunda on a pedestal of sandstone that will match the walls of that historic space. But the case, protected by bulletproof glass, will actually rest on a piece of pegmatite taken from the Hebrides. This incredibly ancient stone (lifted from earth by a Royal Navy helicopter) symbolizes the time before continental drift when North America nestled against the British Isles.

Speaking of it, Osman says: "Thus the design links the past with the present rather than the present with the past; not just the comparatively recent past of the quarrel and separation of two countries or of the 760 years since Magna Carta, but the remote past when they were united three hundred thousand million years ago. It is on a piece of rock from that period, inscribed 'Presented to Congress by the British Parliament in the Bicentennial Year 1976,' that the gift will stand as a perpetual symbol of this unity."

He looks forward to the grand occasion near the

*In his Tudor manor house and workshop opposite, designer Louis Osman considers a part of the display case (see page six). At the far left appear one of Osman's craftsmen and the extraordinary crown they created for Prince Charles's investiture. Osman decided that the Magna Carta gift case should rest on a slab of ancient, symbolic stone from the foggy Hebrides (above).*

precise birthdate of the Declaration of Independence when a ceremonial guard will open the presentation case containing Magna Carta: "Concealed springs help the four strong men open it. As the lid swings, a shimmering of gold and color is exposed, and a sheet of engraved and gold enamel glass rises automatically to be locked vertically in place. The gold words of Magna Carta are suspended as in air."

Osman points out that the ultimate reward of the British gift, as ordered in the Parliamentary resolution, is the raised gold replica of the 5,000-word charter. At first concealed by the document itself, the replica, an integral part of the gold-lined encasing, will remain here after Magna Carta returns to the British Library. The underlying gold tablet is engraved with the words: "Magna Carta 1215. The Great Charter of John, King of England. The foundation of the liberties of Englishmen, from which stem the liberties of the American and British peoples."

With that emblazoned encouragement, grateful Americans visiting the exhibit will be heartened to read the translated text (as follows), and to find in those medieval words intimations of their nation's destiny.

"[W]here the public interest governs, it is a government of laws, and not of men; the interest of a king, or of a party, is another thing—it is a private interest; and where private interest governs, it is a government of men, and not of laws. If, in England, there has ever been such a thing as a government of laws, was it not *magna charta?* and have not

## MAGNA CARTA

This translation by G. R. C. David, D Phil, F R Hist S, is reproduced by permission of the Trustees of the British Museum with certain minor alterations by Sir Ivor Jennings. It sets out to convey the sense rather than the precise wording of the original Latin.

Clauses marked (†) are still valid under the Charter of 1225, but with a few minor amendments. Clauses marked (*) were omitted in all later reissues of the charter. In the charter itself the clauses are not numbered, and the text reads continuously.

JOHN, by the grace of God King of England, Lord of Ireland, Duke of Normandy and Aquitaine, and Count of Anjou, to his archbishops, bishops, abbots, earls, barons, justices, foresters, sheriffs, stewards, servants, and to all his officials and loyal subjects, Greeting.

KNOW THAT BEFORE GOD, for the health of our soul and those of our ancestors and heirs, to the honour of God, the exaltation of the holy Church, and the better ordering of our kingdom, at the advice of our reverend fathers Stephen, archbishop of Canterbury, primate of all England, and cardinal of the holy Roman Church, Henry archbishop of Dublin, William bishop of London, Peter bishop of Winchester, Jocelin bishop of Bath and Glastonbury, Hugh bishop of Lincoln, Walter bishop of Coventry, Benedict bishop of Rochester, Master Pandulf subdeacon and member of the papal household, Brother Aymeric master of the knighthood of the Temple in England, William Marshal earl of Pembroke, William earl of Salisbury, William earl of Warren, William earl of Arundel, Alan de Galloway constable of Scotland, Warin Fitz Gerald, Peter Fitz Herbert, Hubert de Burgh seneschal of Poitou, Hugh de Neville, Matthew Fitz Herbert, Thomas Basset, Alan Basset, Philip Daubeny, Robert de Roppeley, John Marshal, John Fitz Hugh, and other loyal subjects:

†(1) FIRST, THAT WE HAVE GRANTED TO GOD, and by this present charter have confirmed for us and our heirs in perpetuity, that the English Church shall be free, and shall have its rights undiminished, and its liberties unimpaired. That we wish this so to be observed, appears from the fact that of our own free will, before the outbreak of the present dispute between us and our barons, we granted and confirmed by charter the freedom of the Church's elections—a right reckoned to be of the greatest necessity and importance to it—and caused this to be confirmed by Pope Innocent III. This freedom we shall observe ourselves, and desire to be observed in good faith by our heirs in perpetuity.

TO ALL FREE MEN OF OUR KINGDOM we have also granted, for us and our heirs for ever, all the liberties written out below, to have and to keep for them and their heirs, of us and our heirs:

(2) If any earl, baron, or other person that holds lands directly of the Crown, for military service, shall die, and at his death his heir shall be of full age and owe a 'relief', the heir shall have his inheritance on payment of the ancient scale of 'relief'. That is to say, the heir or heirs of an earl shall pay £100 for the entire earl's barony, the heir or heirs of a knight 100s. at most for the entire knight's 'fee', and any man that owes less shall pay less, in accordance with the ancient usage of 'fees'.

(3) But if the heir of such a person is under age and a ward, when he comes of age he shall have his inheritance without 'relief' or fine.

(4) The guardian of the land of an heir who is under age shall take from it only reasonable revenues, customary dues, and feudal services. He shall do this without destruction or damage to men or property. If we have given the guardianship of the land to a sheriff, or to any person answerable to us for the revenues, and he commits destruction or damage, we will exact compensation from him, and the land shall be entrusted to two worthy and prudent men of the same 'fee', who shall be answerable to us for the revenues, or to the person to whom we have assigned them. If we have given or sold to anyone the guardianship of such land, and he causes destruction or damage, he shall lose the guardianship of it, and it shall be handed over to two worthy and prudent men of the same 'fee', who shall be similarly answerable to us.

(5) For so long as a guardian has guardianship of such land, he shall maintain the houses, parks, fish preserves, ponds, mills, and everything else pertaining to it, from the revenues of the land itself. When the heir comes of age, he shall restore the whole land to him, stocked with plough teams and such implements of husbandry as the season demands and the revenues from the land can reasonably bear.

(6) Heirs may be given in marriage, but not to someone of lower social standing. Before a marriage takes place, it shall be made known to the heir's next-of-kin.

(7) At her husband's death, a widow may have her marriage portion and inheritance at once and without trouble. She shall pay nothing for her dower, marriage portion, or any inheritance that she and her husband held jointly on the day of his death. She may remain in her husband's house for forty days after his death, and within this period her dower shall be assigned to her.

54

our kings broken *magna charta* thirty times? Did the law
govern when the law was broken? or was that a government
of men? On the contrary, hath not *magna charta* been as
often repaired by the people? and, the law being so restored,
was it not a government of laws, and not of men?"

–John Adams, 1779

(8) No widow shall be compelled to marry, so long as she wishes to remain without a husband. But she must give security that she will not marry without royal consent, if she holds her lands of the Crown, or without the consent of whatever other lord she may hold them of.

†(9) Neither we nor our officials will seize any land or rent in payment of a debt, so long as the debtor has movable goods sufficient to discharge the debt. A debtor's sureties shall not be distrained upon so long as the debtor himself can discharge his debt. If, for lack of means, the debtor is unable to discharge his debt, his sureties shall be answerable for it. If they so desire, they may have the debtor's lands and rents until they have received satisfaction for the debt that they paid for him, unless the debtor can show that he has settled his obligations to them.

*(10) If anyone who has borrowed a sum of money from Jews dies before the debt has been repaid, his heir shall pay no interest on the debt for so long as he remains under age, irrespective of whom he holds his lands. If such a debt falls into the hands of the crown, it will take nothing except the principal sum specified in the bond.

*(11) If a man dies owing money to Jews, his wife may have her dower and pay nothing towards the debt from it. If he leaves children that are under age, their needs may also be provided for on a scale appropriate to the size of his holding of lands. The debt is to be paid out of the residue, reserving the service due to his fuedal lords. Debts owed to persons other than Jews are to be dealt with similarly.

*(12) No 'scutage' or 'aid' may be levied in our kingdom without general consent, unless it is for the ransom of our person, to make our eldest son a knight, and (once) to marry our eldest daughter. For these purposes only a reasonable 'aid' may be levied. 'Aids' from the city of London are to be treated similarly.

†(13) The city of London shall enjoy all its ancient liberties and free customs, both by land and by water. We also will and grant that all other cities, boroughs, towns, and ports shall enjoy all their liberties and free customs.

*(14) To obtain the general consent for the assessment of an 'aid'—except in the three cases specified above—or a 'scutage', we will cause the archbishops, bishops, abbots, earls, and greater barons to be summoned individually by letter. To those who hold lands directly of us we will cause a general summons to be issued, through the sheriffs and other officials,

to come together on a fixed day (of which at least forty days notice shall be given) and at a fixed place. In all letters of summons, the cause of the summons will be stated. When a summons has been issued, the business appointed for the day shall go forward in accordance with the resolution of those present, even if not all those who were summoned have appeared.

*(15) In future we will allow no one to levy an 'aid' from his free men, except to ransom his person, to make his eldest son a knight, and (once) to marry his eldest daughter. For these purposes only a reasonable 'aid' may be levied.

(16) No man shall be forced to perform more service for a knight's 'fee', or other free holding of land, than is due from it.

(17) Ordinary lawsuits shall not follow the royal court around, but shall be held in a fixed place.

(18) Inquests of *novel disseisin, mort d'ancestor,* and *darrein presentment* shall be taken only in their proper county court. We ourselves, or in our absence abroad our chief justice, will send two justices to each county four times a year, and these justices, with four knights of the county elected by the county itself, shall hold the assizes in the county court, on the day and in the place where the court meets.

(19) If any assizes cannot be taken on the day of the county court, as many knights and freeholders shall afterwards remain behind, of those who have attended the court, as will suffice for the administration of justice, having regard to the volume of business to be done.

†(20) For a trivial offence, a free man shall be fined only in proportion to the degree of his offence, and for a serious offence correspondingly, but not so heavily as to deprive him of his livelihood. In the same way, a merchant shall be spared his merchandise, and a husbandman the implements of his husbandry, if they fall upon the mercy of a royal court. None of these fines shall be imposed except by the assessment of reputable men of the neighbourhood.

†(21) Earls and barons shall be fined only by their equals, and in proportion to the gravity of their offence.

†(22) A fine imposed upon the lay property of a clerk in holy orders shall be assessed upon the same principles, without reference to the value of his ecclesiastical benefice.

†(23) No town or person shall be forced to build bridges over rivers except those with an ancient obligation to do so.

*"That all power was originally in the People—that all the powers of Government are derived from them—that all power, which they have not disposed of, still continues theirs—are maxims of the English Constitution, which, we presume, will not be disputed."*
—James Wilson, 1776

(24) No sheriff, constable, coroners, or other royal officials are to hold lawsuits that should be held by the royal justices.

*(25) Every county, hundred, wapentake, and tithing shall remain at its ancient rent, without increase, except the royal demesne manors.

(26) If at the death of a man who holds a lay 'fee' of the Crown, a sheriff or royal official produces royal letters patent of summons for a debt due to the Crown, it shall be lawful for them to seize and list movable goods found in the lay 'fee' of the dead man to the value of the debt, as assessed by worthy men. Nothing shall be removed until the whole debt is paid, when the residue shall be given over to the executors to carry out the dead man's will. If no debt is due to the Crown, all the movable goods shall be regarded as the property of the dead man, except the reasonable shares of his wife and children.

*(27) If a free man dies intestate, his movable goods are to be distributed by his next-of-kin and friends, under the supervision of the Church. The rights of his debtors are to be preserved.

(28) No constable or other royal official shall take corn or other movable goods from any man without immediate payment, unless the seller voluntarily offers postponement of this.

(29) No constable may compel a knight to pay money for castleguard if the knight is willing to undertake the guard in person, or with reasonable excuse to supply some other fit man to do it. A knight taken or sent on military service shall be excused from castleguard for the period of this service.

(30) No sheriff, royal official, or other person shall take horses or carts for transport from any free man, without his consent.

(31) Neither we nor any royal official will take wood for our castle, or for any other purpose, without the consent of the owner.

(32) We will not keep the lands of people convicted of felony in our hand for longer than a year and a day, after which they shall be returned to the lords of the 'fees' concerned.

†(33) All fish-weirs shall be removed from the Thames, the Medway, and throughout the whole of England, except on the sea coast.

(34) The writ called *precipe* shall not in future be issued to anyone in respect of any holding of land, if a free man could thereby be deprived of the right of trial in his own lord's court.

(35) There shall be standard measures of wine, ale, and corn (the London quarter), throughout the kingdom. There shall also be a standard width of dyed cloth, russett, and haberject, namely two ells within the selvedges. Weights are to be standardised similarly.

(36) In future nothing shall be paid or accepted for the issue of a writ of inquisition of life or limbs. It shall be given *gratis*, and not refused.

(37) If a man holds land of the Crown by 'fee-farm', 'socage', or 'burgage', and also holds land of someone else for knight's service, we will not have guardianship of his heir, nor of the land that belongs to the other person's 'fee', by virtue of the 'fee-farm', 'socage', or 'burgage', unless the 'fee-farm' owes knight's service. We will not have the guardianship of a man's heir, or of land that he holds of someone else, by reason of any small property that he may hold of the Crown for a service of knives, arrows, or the like.

(38) In future no official shall place a man on trial upon his own unsupported statement, without producing credible witnesses to the truth of it.

†(39) No free man shall be seized or imprisoned, or stripped of his rights or possessions, or outlawed or exiled, or deprived of his standing in any other way, nor will we proceed with force against him, or send others to do so, except by the lawful judgement of his equals or by the law of the land.

†(40) To no one will we sell, to no one deny or delay right or justice.

†(41) All merchants may enter or leave England unharmed and without fear, and may stay or travel within it, by land or water, for purposes of trade, free from all illegal exactions, in accordance with ancient and lawful customs. This, however, does not apply in time of war to merchants from a country that is at war with us. Any such merchants found in our country at the outbreak of war shall be detained without injury to their persons or property, until we or our chief justice have discovered how our own merchants are being treated in the country at war with us. If our own merchants are safe they shall be safe too.

*(42) In future it shall be lawful for any man to leave and return to our kingdom unharmed and without fear, by land or water, preserving his allegiance to us, except in time of war, for some short period, for the common benefit of the realm. People that have been imprisoned or outlawed in accordance with the law of the land, people from a country that is at war with us, and merchants—who shall be dealt with as stated above—are excepted from this provision.

(43) If a man holds lands of any 'escheat' such as the 'honour' of Wallingford, Nottingham, Boulogne, Lancaster or of other 'escheats' in our hand that are baronies, at his death his heir shall give us only the 'relief' and service that he would have made to the baron, had the barony been in the baron's hand. We will hold the 'escheat' in the same manner as the baron held it.

†(44) People who live outside the forest need not in future appear before the royal justices of the forest in answer to general summonses, unless they are actually involved in proceedings or are sureties for someone who has been seized for a forest offence.

*(45) We will appoint as justices, constables, sheriffs, or other officials, only men that know the law of the realm and are minded to keep it well.

(46) All barons who have founded abbeys, and have charters of English kings or ancient tenure as evidence of this, may have guardianship of them when there is no abbot, as is their due.

(47) †All forests that have been created in our reign shall at once be disafforested.† River-banks that have been enclosed in our reign shall be treated similarly.

*(48) All evil customs relating to forests and warrens, foresters, warreners, sheriffs and their servants, or river-banks and their wardens, are at once to be investigated in every county by twelve sworn knights of the county, and within forty days of their enquiry the evil customs are to be abolished completely and irrevocably. But we, or our chief justice if we are not in England, are first to be informed.

*(49) We will at once return all hostages and charters delivered up to us by Englishmen as security for peace or for loyal service.

*(50) We will remove completely from their offices the kinsmen of Gerard de Athée, and in future they shall hold no offices in England. The people in question are Engelard de Cigogné, Peter Guy, and Andrew de Chanceaux, Guy de Cigogné, Geoffrey de Martigny and his brothers, Philip Marc and his brothers, with Geoffrey his nephew, and all their followers.

*(51) As soon as peace is restored, we will remove from the kingdom all the foreign knights, bowmen, their attendants, and the mercenaries that have come to it, to its harm, with horses and arms.

*(52) To any man whom we have deprived or dispossessed of lands, castles, liberties, or rights, without the lawful judgement of his equals, we will at once restore these. In cases of dispute the matter shall be resolved by the judgement of the twenty-five barons referred to below in the clause for securing the peace (#61). In cases, however, where a man was deprived or dispossessed of something without the lawful judgement of his equals by our father King Henry or our brother King Richard, and it remains in our hands or is held by others under our warranty, we shall have respite for the period commonly allowed to Crusaders, unless a lawsuit had been begun, or an enquiry had been made at our order, before we took the Cross as a Crusader. On our return from the Crusade, or if we abandon it, we will at once render justice in full.

*(53) We shall have similar respite in rendering justice in connexion with forests that are to be disafforested, or to remain forests, when these were first afforested by our father Henry or our brother Richard; with the guardianship of lands in another person's 'fee', when we have hitherto had this by virtue of a 'fee' held of us for knight's service by a third party; and with abbeys founded in another person's 'fee', in which the lord of the 'fee' claims to own a right. On our return from the Crusade, or if we abandon it, we will at once do full justice to complaints about these matters.

(54) No one shall be arrested or imprisoned on the appeal of a woman for the death of any person except her husband.

*(55) All fines that have been given to us unjustly and against the law of the land, and all fines that we have exacted unjustly, shall be entirely remitted or the matter decided by a majority judgement of the twenty-five barons referred to below in the clause for securing the peace (#61) together with Stephen, archbishop of Canterbury, if he can be present, and such others as he wishes to bring with him. If the archbishop cannot be present, proceedings shall continue without him, provided that if any of the twenty-five barons has been involved in a similar suit himself, his judgement shall be set aside, and someone else chosen and sworn in his place, as a substitute for the single occasion, by the rest of the twenty-five.

(56) If we have deprived or dispossessed any Welshmen of lands, liberties, or anything else in England or in Wales, without the lawful judgement of their equals, these are at once to be returned to them. A dispute on this point shall be determined in the Marches by the judgement of equals. English law shall apply to holdings of land in England, Welsh law to those in Wales, and the law of the Marches to those in the Marches. The Welsh shall treat us and ours in the same way.

*(57) In cases where a Welshman was deprived or dispossessed of anything, without the lawful judgement of his equals, by our father King Henry or our brother King Richard, and it remains in our hands or is held by others under our warranty, we shall have respite for the period commonly allowed to Crusaders, unless a lawsuit had been begun, or an enquiry had been made at our order, before we took the Cross as a Crusader. But on our return from the Crusade, or if we abandon it, we will at once do full justice according to the laws of Wales and the said regions.

*(58) We will at once return the son of Llywelyn, all Welsh hostages, and the charters delivered to us as security for the peace.

*(59) With regard to the return of the sisters and hostages of Alexander, king of Scotland, his liberties and his rights, we will treat him in the same way as our other barons of England, unless it appears from the charters that we hold from his father William, formerly king of Scotland, that he should be treated otherwise. This matter shall be resolved by the judgement of his equals in our court.

(60) All these customs and liberties that we have granted shall be observed in our kingdom in so far as concerns our own relations with our subjects. Let all men of our kingdom, whether clergy or laymen, observe them similarly in their relations with their own men.

*(61) SINCE WE HAVE GRANTED ALL THESE THINGS for God, for the better ordering of our kingdom, and to allay the discord that has arisen between us and our barons, and since we desire that they shall be enjoyed in their entirety, with lasting strength, for ever, we give and grant to the barons the following security:

*The barons shall elect twenty-five of their number to keep, and cause to be observed with all their might, the peace and liberties granted and confirmed to them by this charter.*

*If we, our chief justice, our officials, or any of our servants offend in any respect against any man, or transgress any of the articles of the peace or of this security, and the offence is made known to four of the said twenty-five barons, they shall come to us—or in our absence from the kingdom to the chief justice—to declare it and claim immediate redress. If we, or in our absence abroad the chief justice, make no redress within forty days, reckoning from the day on which the offence was declared to us or to him, the four barons shall refer the matter to the rest of the twenty-five barons, who may distrain upon and assail us in every way possible, with the support of the whole community of the land, by seizing our castles, lands, possessions, or anything else saving only our own person and those of the queen and our children, until they have secured such redress as they have determined upon. Having secured the redress, they may then resume their normal obedience to us.*

*Any man who so desires may take an oath to obey the commands of the twenty-five barons for the achievement of these ends, and to join with them in assailing us to the utmost of his power. We give public and free permission to take this oath to any man who so desires, and at no time will we prohibit any man from taking it. Indeed, we will compel any of our subjects who are unwilling to take it to swear it at our command.*

*If one of the twenty-five barons dies or leaves the country, or is prevented in any other way from discharging his duties, the rest of them shall choose another baron in his place, at their discretion, who shall be duly sworn in as they were.*

*In the event of disagreement among the twenty-five barons on any matter referred to them for decision, the verdict of the majority present shall have the same validity as a unanimous verdict of the whole twenty-five, whether these were all present or some of those summoned were unwilling or unable to appear.*

*The twenty-five barons shall swear to obey all the above articles faithfully, and shall cause them to be obeyed by others to the best of their power.*

*We will not seek to procure from anyone, either by our own efforts or those of a third party, anything by which any part of these concessions or liberties might be revoked or diminished. Should such a thing be procured, it shall be null and void and we will at no time take use of it, either ourselves or through a third party.*

*(62) We have remitted and pardoned fully to all men any ill-will, hurt or grudges that have arisen between us and our subjects, whether clergy or laymen, since the beginning of the dispute. We have in addition remitted fully, and for our own part have also pardoned, to all clergy and laymen any offences committed as a result of the said dispute between Easter in the sixteenth year of our reign (*i.e.* 1215) and the restoration of peace.

In addition we have caused letters patent to be made for the barons, bearing witness to this security and to the concessions set out above, over the seals of Stephen archbishop of Canterbury, Henry archbishop of Dublin, the other bishops named above, and Master Pandulf.

*(63) IT IS ACCORDINGLY OUR WISH AND COMMAND that the English Church shall be free, and that men in our kingdom shall have and keep all these liberties, rights, and concessions, well and peaceably in their fulness and entirety for them and their heirs, of us and our heirs, in all things and all places for ever.

Both we and the barons have sworn that all this shall be observed in good faith and without deceit. Witness the abovementioned people and many others.

Given by our hand in the meadow that is called Runnymede, between Windsor and Staines, on the fifteenth day of June in the seventeenth year of our reign (*i.e.* 1215: *the new regnal year began on 28 May*).

*The magnificent British Bicentennial*
*gift is viewed through etched glass, above.*

# SUGGESTIONS FOR FURTHER READING

A series authorized by the Magna Carta Commission of Virginia to celebrate the 750th anniversary of Magna Carta, published by the University Press of Virginia, is very helpful to the reader without the time or inclination to consult longer works. The most important of these booklets are: A. E. Dick Howard, *Magna Carta: Text and Commentary* (1964); J. C. Holt, *The Making of Magna Carta* (1965); Arthur L. Goodhart, *"Law of the Land"* (1966); Maurice Ashley, *Magna Carta in the Seventeenth Century* (1965); Doris M. Stenton, *After Runnymede: Magna Carta in the Middle Ages* (1965); and Daniel J. Meador, *Habeas Corpus and Magna Carta* (1966). Invaluable for the light that it throws on the influence of Magna Carta in America is A. E. Dick Howard, *The Road from Runnymede: Magna Carta and Constitutionalism in America* (Charlottesville, 1968).

One of the most useful books for the general reader wishing to learn more about Magna Carta, its meaning and its history, is William F. Swindler, *Magna Carta, Legend and Legacy* (Indianapolis, 1965). He provides a useful bibliography and notes on recent scholarship. An older and classic work is William S. McKechnie, *Magna Carta: A Commentary on the Great Charter of King John* (Glasgow, 1905). McKechnie gives the Latin text and a translation of Magna Carta, and discusses the reissues and confirmations. Although a few of his generalizations have been modified by more recent scholarship, his work remains a standard authority.

A more recent treatise on Magna Carta, paralleling Swindler's book but written from the English point of view is J. C. Holt, *Magna Carta* (Cambridge, 1965).

A highly readable book, entertaining as well as informative about Sir Edward Coke, is Catherine Drinker Bowen, *The Lion and the Throne: The Life and Times of Sir Edward Coke* (Boston, 1956). Mrs. Bowen includes a detailed bibliography of Coke and his influence.

Valuable information about the history of the period of King John will be found in J. C. Holt, *King John* (London, 1963), Sidney Painter, *The Reign of King John* (Baltimore, 1949), and W. L. Warren, *King John* (New York, 1961). Useful and authoritative is Sir Frederick Pollock and Frederic W. Maitland, *The History of English Law before the Time of Edward I* (Cambridge, 1952).

# CREDITS AND ACKNOWLEDGMENTS

The editors of this book gratefully trace its origins to the decision of the executive committee of the United States Capitol Historical Society to publish an American explanatory text on Magna Carta, upon a request for aid from the British Embassy in Washington. Under the leadership of president Fred Schwengel, the Society fostered the book's development, being joined in that endeavor by the American Revolution Bicentennial Administration (which graciously agreed to fund the project) and the Supreme Court Historical Society. Among those at the Society who provided unstinting assistance were Oliver Patton, who accepted responsibility for the book's production, and editors William Maury and Maier Fox. William Blue and his staff at ARBA helped immeasurably to bring the book into existence, as did William Press of the Supreme Court Historical Society.

In addition to expressing appreciation to the British Ambassador, the Honorable Sir Peter Ramsbotham, K.C.M.G., the editors would like to thank the following people whose valiant work made this book possible: Merrick Baker-Bates and Diana Fortescue, the British Embassy, Washington; Janet Backhouse and Michael Borrie, the British Library, London; D.A. Pearce, M.B.E., the Foreign Office, London; and Bob Salthouse, the Central Office of Information, London.

# ILLUSTRATIONS

Cover top: By John Hamilton Mortimer, Folger Shakespeare Library, btm: By Robert Edge Pine and John Savage, Historical Society of Pennsylvania. Front endsheet: Cotton Ms. Augustus II, fo. 106, BL. 4: COI. 5: Robert S. Oakes, National Geographic Society. 6 top: Jeremy Whitaker, btm: By Paul Revere, LC. 7: American Revolution Bicentennial Administration. 8: Jeremy Whitaker. 10: Commonwealth of Massachusetts. 11 top: By Percy Moran, Pilgrim Hall Museum, Plymouth, Massachusetts, btm: Jamestown Foundation. 12 top: By John Hamilton Mortimer, Folger Shakespeare Library, btm: U.S. Capitol Historical Society. 13 top: COI, ctr: British Museum, btm: BL. 14 both: COI. 16: Paul Kelner. 18: Historical Society of Pennsylvania. 19: By special permission of the town of Bayeux. 20: Cotton Ms. B iv, fo. 59, BL. 21 both: COI. 22: Royal Ms. 2A xxii, fo. 220, BL. 23 left: Royal Ms. 20A ii, fo. 8, BL, right: Add Ms. 42130, fo. 202b, BL. 24: Cotton Ms. Claudius D ii, fo. 70, BL. 25 left: Harley Ms. 5102, fo. 32, BL, right: British Museum. 26: COI. 27 top: Cotton Ms. Claudius D ii 70, fo. 133, BL, btm: COI. 28: Cotton Ms. Vitellius A xiii, fo.

5b, BL. 30: Wriothesley Ms., By permission of Her Majesty the Queen. 31 left, ctr: COI, right: British Museum. 32: By Robert White, Folger Shakespeare Library. 33: By Marcus Gheeraerts, National Portrait Gallery, London. 34 left: National Portrait Gallery, London, right. British Museum. 35: The Mansell Collection. 36: COI. 37 left: Earl Gregg Swem Library, College of William and Mary, right, btm: Thomas Williams. 38: By Edward Hicks, Abby Aldrich Rockefeller Folk Art Collection, Williamsburg, Virginia. 40: By George Cook, Virginia Historical Society. 41 left: LC, right: Haverford College. 42: Metropolitan Museum of Art. 43 left: LC, right: Bettman Archive. 44: John Carter Brown Library, Brown University. 45: By Charles Willson Peale, Historical Society of Pennsylvania. 46 left: By John Singleton Copley, Boston Museum of Fine Arts, right: By Charles Fevret de Saint-Memin, Worcester Art Museum, btm: By Benjamin Blythe, Massachusetts Historical Society. 47 both: LC. 48-49: By Robert Edge Pine and Edward Savage, Pennsylvania Historical Society. 50: Jeremy Whitaker. 52 top left, right: Jeremy Whitaker, btm left: COI. 53: Louis B. Osman. 59 both: Jeremy Whitaker. Back endsheet: National Archives.

## STAFF FOR THIS BOOK

Editor: Russell Bourne
Text and Picture Research: Christine Bowie
Editorial Assistant: Karen E. Maury
Design and Production: Wickham & Associates
Index: John Kimball
Consultant:  William F. Swindler
             John Marshall Professor of Law
             College of William and Mary

Printed by Judd and Detweiler, Inc.

# INDEX

# In CONGRESS, July 4, 1776.

## The unanimous Declaration of the thirteen united States of America.

When in the Course of human events, it becomes necessary for one people to dissolve the political bands which have connected them with another, and to assume among the powers of the earth, the separate and equal station to which the Laws of Nature and of Nature's God entitle them, a decent respect to the opinions of mankind requires that they should declare the causes which impel them to the separation.

We hold these truths to be self-evident, that all men are created equal, that they are endowed by their Creator with certain unalienable Rights, that among these are Life, Liberty and the pursuit of Happiness.—That to secure these rights, Governments are instituted among Men, deriving their just powers from the consent of the governed,—That whenever any Form of Government becomes destructive of these ends, it is the Right of the People to alter or to abolish it, and to institute new Government, laying its foundation on such principles and organizing its powers in such form, as to them shall seem most likely to effect their Safety and Happiness. Prudence, indeed, will dictate that Governments long established should not be changed for light and transient causes; and accordingly all experience hath shewn, that mankind are more disposed to suffer, while evils are sufferable, than to right themselves by abolishing the forms to which they are accustomed. But when a long train of abuses and usurpations, pursuing invariably the same Object evinces a design to reduce them under absolute Despotism, it is their right, it is their duty, to throw off such Government, and to provide new Guards for their future security.—Such has been the patient sufferance of these Colonies; and such is now the necessity which constrains them to alter their former Systems of Government. The history of the present King of Great Britain is a history of repeated injuries and usurpations, all having in direct object the establishment of an absolute Tyranny over these States. To prove this, let Facts be submitted to a candid world.

He has refused his Assent to Laws, the most wholesome and necessary for the public good.
He has forbidden his Governors to pass Laws of immediate and pressing importance, unless suspended in their operation till his Assent should be obtained; and when so suspended, he has utterly neglected to attend to them.
He has refused to pass other Laws for the accommodation of large districts of people, unless those people would relinquish the right of Representation in the Legislature, a right inestimable to them and formidable to tyrants only.
He has called together legislative bodies at places unusual, uncomfortable, and distant from the depository of their Public Records, for the sole purpose of fatiguing them into compliance with his measures.
He has dissolved Representative Houses repeatedly, for opposing with manly firmness his invasions on the rights of the people.
He has refused for a long time, after such dissolutions, to cause others to be elected; whereby the Legislative powers, incapable of Annihilation, have returned to the People at large for their exercise; the State remaining in the mean time exposed to all the dangers of invasion from without, and convulsions within.
He has endeavoured to prevent the population of these States; for that purpose obstructing the Laws for Naturalization of Foreigners; refusing to pass others to encourage their migrations hither, and raising the conditions of new Appropriations of Lands.
He has obstructed the Administration of Justice, by refusing his Assent to Laws for establishing Judiciary powers.
He has made Judges dependent on his Will alone, for the tenure of their offices, and the amount and payment of their salaries.
He has erected a multitude of New Offices, and sent hither swarms of Officers to harrass our people, and eat out their substance.
He has kept among us, in times of peace, Standing Armies without the Consent of our legislatures.
He has affected to render the Military independent of and superior to the Civil power.
He has combined with others to subject us to a jurisdiction foreign to our constitution, and unacknowledged by our laws; giving his Assent to their Acts of pretended Legislation:
For Quartering large bodies of armed troops among us:
For protecting them, by a mock Trial, from punishment for any Murders which they should commit on the Inhabitants of these States:
For cutting off our Trade with all parts of the world:
For imposing Taxes on us without our Consent:
For depriving us in many cases, of the benefits of Trial by jury:
For transporting us beyond Seas to be tried for pretended offences:
For abolishing the free System of English Laws in a neighbouring Province, establishing therein an Arbitrary government, and enlarging its Boundaries so as to render it at once an example and fit instrument for introducing the same absolute rule into these Colonies:
For taking away our Charters, abolishing our most valuable Laws, and altering fundamentally the Forms of our Governments:
For suspending our own Legislatures, and declaring themselves invested with power to legislate for us in all cases whatsoever.
He has abdicated Government here, by declaring us out of his Protection and waging War against us.
He has plundered our seas, ravaged our Coasts, burnt our towns, and destroyed the lives of our people.
He is at this time transporting large Armies of foreign Mercenaries to compleat the works of death, desolation and tyranny, already begun with circumstances of Cruelty & perfidy scarcely paralleled in the most barbarous ages, and totally unworthy the Head of a civilized nation.
He has constrained our fellow Citizens taken Captive on the high Seas to bear Arms against their Country, to become the executioners of their friends and Brethren, or to fall themselves by their Hands.
He has excited domestic insurrections amongst us, and has endeavoured to bring on the inhabitants of our frontiers, the merciless Indian Savages, whose known rule of warfare, is an undistinguished destruction of all ages, sexes and conditions.

In every stage of these Oppressions We have Petitioned for Redress in the most humble terms: Our repeated Petitions have been answered only by repeated injury. A Prince, whose character is thus marked by every act which may define a Tyrant, is unfit to be the ruler of a free people.

Nor have We been wanting in attentions to our British brethren. We have warned them from time to time of attempts by their legislature to extend an unwarrantable jurisdiction over us. We have reminded them of the circumstances of our emigration and settlement here. We have appealed to their native justice and magnanimity, and we have conjured them by the ties of our common kindred to disavow these usurpations, which, would inevitably interrupt our connections and correspondence. They too have been deaf to the voice of justice and of consanguinity. We must, therefore, acquiesce in the necessity, which denounces our Separation, and hold them, as we hold the rest of mankind, Enemies in War, in Peace Friends.

We, therefore, the Representatives of the united States of America, in General Congress, Assembled, appealing to the Supreme Judge of the world for the rectitude of our intentions, do, in the Name, and by Authority of the good People of these Colonies, solemnly publish and declare, That these United Colonies are, and of Right ought to be Free and Independent States; that they are Absolved from all Allegiance to the British Crown, and that all political connection between them and the State of Great Britain, is and ought to be totally dissolved; and that as Free and Independent States, they have full Power to levy War, conclude Peace, contract Alliances, establish Commerce, and to do all other Acts and Things which Independent States may of right do. And for the support of this Declaration, with a firm reliance on the protection of divine Providence, we mutually pledge to each other our Lives, our Fortunes and our sacred Honor.

John Hancock

Button Gwinnett
Lyman Hall
Geo Walton

Wm Hooper
Joseph Hewes
John Penn

Edward Rutledge
Thos Heyward Junr.
Thomas Lynch Junr.
Arthur Middleton

Samuel Chase
Wm Paca
Thos Stone
Charles Carroll of Carrollton

George Wythe
Richard Henry Lee
Th Jefferson
Benj Harrison
Thos Nelson jr.
Francis Lightfoot Lee
Carter Braxton

Robt Morris
Benjamin Rush
Benja. Franklin
John Morton
Geo Clymer
Jas. Smith
Geo. Taylor
James Wilson
Geo. Ross
Caesar Rodney
Geo Read
Tho M:Kean

Wm Floyd
Phil. Livingston
Frans. Lewis
Lewis Morris
Richd. Stockton
Jno Witherspoon
Fras. Hopkinson
John Hart
Abra Clark

Josiah Bartlett
Wm Whipple
Saml Adams
John Adams
Robt Treat Paine
Elbridge Gerry
Step. Hopkins
William Ellery
Roger Sherman
Sam. Huntington
Wm Williams
Oliver Wolcott
Matthew Thornton

AMERICAN REVOLUTION BICENTENNIAL 1776-1976 ™